DANCES
OF OUR PIONEERS

DANCES
OF
OUR PIONEERS

Collected by GRACE L. RYAN
Department of Physical Education,
Central State Teachers College,
Mt. Pleasant, Michigan

Music Arrangements by ROBERT T. BENFORD

Illustrations by BROOKS EMERSON

Established in 1838

A. S. BARNES & COMPANY · NEW YORK

PRINTED IN THE UNITED STATES OF AMERICA

This book is lovingly dedicated to my aunts, ANNA and NORA RYAN.

FOREWORD

WITH INCREASED EMPHASIS upon recreation and with the recent widespread interest in American folk culture has come a demand for the dances of our pioneers. There has been a revival of these dances in rural areas throughout the country. In urban centers recreation leaders are giving them a definite place in their programs.

The pioneer dances are attractive for several reasons. The formations in groups, circles, and squares, with frequent changes of partners, make them truly social. They are hilarious enough to make good wholesome fun, especially if conducted by experienced "callers" whose "calls" are humorous and original. They vary in difficulty from simple to complex figures so that dancers soon do them well enough to gain satisfaction, yet hold interest over long periods as the intricacy of the patterns increases. Finally, they are so vigorous that they give real physical activity.

The dances may be used with mixed groups of nearly all ages. In the elementary schools they make interesting activity in simplified form as part of pioneer life studies; in the junior high schools they are valuable in a co-educational social program and as a background for other social dancing; and with adults they provide excellent recreation. American country dance clubs are becoming increasingly popular in high schools, colleges, and community groups.

The figures are different in the various sections of the United States, but the fundamentals are similar in most areas. The "calls" vary with the "caller" and the locale. The majority of the dances of this book were collected in the Middle West, although a few are from the Rocky Mountains and the Eastern Appalachians. I have presented them as I have found them being done in the country.

I wish to express my sincere appreciation to my many friends for their interest and help in making this collection. I desire especially to mention Mrs. Frances Bliss, Miss Antoinette Faucher, Mr. John Moriarity, Mr. Lee Miller, Mr. E. V. Beeve, and Mr. Alva Asbury for contributions they have made; Mr. Robert Benford, Miss Dora Silver, Mrs. Myrle Thiers, and Miss Edith Nelson for assistance with the music; Mr. Brooks Emerson for illustrations.

PREFACE

WHEN MISS RYAN so graciously asked me to write the preface for her book, *Dances of Our Pioneers*, I thought of a ballroom scene a year or so ago when I was rather hesitantly drawn from a seat along the sidelines to make up the proper number of persons for a set in the square dance that was about to begin. Miss Ryan was the leader and demonstrated the steps that the dancers were to follow. Soon the floor was filled with couples moving to the swing of the music and the instructions that she called. Enjoyment began to appear in the faces of participants and onlookers alike. Unfamiliarity and awkwardness were forgotten. It did not matter that mistakes were made. It was all good fun.

In writing of Miss Ryan's book, therefore, I feel as though I can already claim a friendship with some of the dances in it. And I know that many, many other people have enjoyed the various square dances, reels, circle dances, and couple dances that she so clearly describes therein.

For many years, Miss Ryan has been indefatigable in tracing the pioneer dances that are still found in the rural sections of our country. These she has written up so that they now have the permanence of the written word. With the recording of these dances many more people are being taught to enjoy them. This is a distinct service to the recreation movement of today.

It has been noticeable in recent years that the folk dances have grown in popularity. One reason probably, apart from their own appeal, is the fact that the ballroom dance has tended to lose its sociability and become an aggregation of "isolated pairs." Consequently, the answer to a felt need has been found in the "mixer" aspect of the pioneer dance. It breaks down formal reserve and allows the "get acquainted" spirit to be fostered. Its appeal is nowhere more evident than in the fact that some of the latest ballroom novelties are, in reality, no more or less than some combination of tuneful music and folk cadence dressed up in modern garb. There surely is worthwhileness in activity in which everyone is made to feel so gay and friendly.

The folk dance makes the past live again. Eager school boys and girls and grown men and women thrill to some racial urge as they participate in the rich heritage of our American folk games. These express the venturesome spirit and physical vigor of our pioneer forebears. And, if it is important for school children to study history to know how people throughout the ages have lived and acted, how fitting an accompaniment that these same children should participate in the spirit of the past and this is the emotional experience that they share when they dance and engage in the communal festivities so close to the lives of other peoples and of other times.

If this contact with the spirit of the past and the spontaneous fun that has already been mentioned are two important values of the folk dance, there is still a further value in the democratizing spirit that is created among the members of the group. There is social significance in this "we" feeling, in this breakdown of reserve, of caste, of race. The folk dance is truly leavening and for that reason it is an activity which takes on a universal aspect and performs a democratic function. Any activity that can make for friendliness and happiness and, at the same time, help produce healthy and graceful bodies is rendering a major service to the institution of democracy.

For these many reasons, the physical education and recreation movement of today should be grateful to Miss Grace Ryan for assembling this valuable collection of dances. The *Dances of Our Pioneers* has the advantage of being written by an author who understands the problems of teaching and of recreational leadership as well as those special problems of the rural community. This book will never grow old because its contents link the past with the present and future. The folk dance embodies the universal spirit that lives in mankind.

ELMER D. MITCHELL
Professor of Physical Education,
University of Michigan.

CONTENTS

MUSIC

ILLUSTRATIONS

DANCES
OF OUR PIONEERS

DEFINITIONS
OF TERMS

Allemande Left

May be given while couples are in quadrille or circle formation, and all couples execute it at the same time in the same manner. The boy turns to the girl at his left, takes her left hand in his, puts his right hand at her back, and turns her once around, both falling back to places.

Allemande Right

This also is given while couples are in quadrille or circle formation. Each boy passes behind his partner to the girl on his right, takes her right hand in his and turns her once around. He returns to his own partner, takes her left hand in his and turns her once around to place.

Balance

This term has a variety of meanings:
1. Step right on count 1; swing left foot across right and point, count "and"; rise on toes, count 2; lower heels, count "and."
2. Dancers take two steps toward each other, and two steps back—4 counts.
3. Balance Four. This is executed where two couples are facing each other. Partners join both hands and chassé, or

walk across to opposite place, turn about and return in the same manner to place.

4. Balance to the next couple: Partners join inside hands and chassé or walk to a position in front of the next couple at their right.

5. Balance across. Same as "Balance four."

Cast Off

Couples are arranged in contra-dance formation when this term is used. The active couple advances one place nearer the foot of the set by merely stepping behind one couple to a position below them.

$$\text{Head} \quad G^1 \quad G^2 \searrow \quad G^3 \quad G^4 \quad \text{Foot}$$
$$B_1 \quad \underset{\nearrow}{B_2} \quad B_3 \quad B_4$$

Chassé

The term has reference to a movement which is used in all country dancing; namely, a sliding step, keeping one foot ahead of the other—slide-close, slide-close, etc.

Contra-Dance Formation

Couples are arranged in two lines facing; generally with the girls on one side and the boys on the other.

$$G^1 \quad G^2 \quad G^3 \quad G^4 \quad G^5 \quad G^6$$
$$B_1 \quad B_2 \quad B_3 \quad B_4 \quad B_5 \quad B_6$$

Do-Si-Do or Dos-á-Dos

Dancers facing. They advance and pass right shoulders continuing on around each other back to back, returning to original places.

Forward and Back

Dancers move forward four counts and back.

GRAND CHAIN

See "Grand Right and Left."

GRAND RIGHT AND LEFT

The dancers are in quadrille or circle formation. Partners face and give right hands to each other. Passing by, each gives left hand to the next dancer, right to the next, and so on around the circle until all have reached original places. As partners meet each other half-way around the circle they salute.

GRAND RIGHT AND LEFT WITH AN ELBOW SWING

Same as grand right and left, only dancers hook elbows instead of joining hands, and swing completely around each time.

HONOR PARTNERS

Partners bow to each other.

HONOR CORNERS

The dancers are in quadrille formation. The girl of each couple bows to the dancer at her right, and the boy to the dancer at his left.

LADIES CHAIN OR LADIES CHANGE

Two couples facing. The girls advance toward each other and give right hands; passing by, each gives her left hand to the opposite boy who turns her half around. Repeat, returning to original partner. (When the girls do not return, the figure is called "Ladies Half Chain.")

LADIES DOUBLE CHAIN

The four girls of the set advance to the center, join right hands in a "star" formation, circle half and give left hand to opposite boy, who turns the girl half around.

Repeat, returning to own partners.

PAY ADDRESS

Same as "Honor Partners."

PROMENADE

Girls take partner's right arm. Couples advance around the set with walking or chassé steps. Sometimes dancers use the two-step for the promenade. In this case twice the amount of music is used.

PROMENADE ACROSS

Same as "Balance Four."

PROMENADE AWAY

Dancers leave the floor at the end of a dance.

QUADRILLE FORMATION

Four couples facing a hollow square.

RIGHT AND LEFT

This is executed by two couples facing each other. They advance with walking or "chassé" steps to meet each other and pass through, the boys going outside.

After passing through, the boy of each couple takes his lady's left hand in his and turns her about. The couples pass through again, returning to original places. Sometimes when a couple is advancing around the set, they right and left half, that is: pass through once only.

RIGHT AND LEFT EIGHT

Is the same as "Right and Left" except that eight people instead of four execute the figure and make a floor pattern which is twice as long as in "Right and Left."

SALUTE PARTNERS

Same as "Honor Partners."

SET

The "set" has reference to the dance formation. For instance, a quadrille or a contra-dance formation may each be spoken of as a "set."

STAR WITH RIGHT HAND

Four people join right hands and circle either with walking or "chassé" steps.

STAR WITH LEFT HAND

Same as "Star with Right Hand," only join left hands and turn the opposite direction.

STAR WITH BOTH HANDS

Two people face and join both hands. Two others join both hands over the joined hands of the first two. Circle left.

SWING PARTNERS

Boy takes girl in regular dance position, holding her at his right. The "swing" is a whirl, partners keeping right feet side by side, pushing with left foot. Sometimes called the "Buzz Step."

QUADRILLES
OR
SQUARE DANCES

IN MOST COMMUNITIES the square dance has been more popular than dances in contra-dance formation and more of them are being done at the present time. They were originally done in five parts but are now found in three parts and in some places only two. These parts are called changes. The music stops at the end of each, and a new tune is used for the following change. To dance a set means to dance three changes. Since the first change is the introductory part of the dance it does not vary a great deal. Sometimes callers will use the same first change with each dance. The second change has great variety and is the most interesting figure of the quadrille. The third change, sometimes called the "Jig Figure," is the fastest of the three changes and almost always has a good deal of "swing partners" in it. The caller does not use the three changes in any regular combination, but uses any first change, second change, and jig figure together. Naturally there is a great deal of originality shown by the callers and no two are exactly alike either in the call itself or in the manner of calling.

In this book I have six quadrilles with the three parts grouped together. In addition, I have several first, second, and third changes which may be used in any grouping which one desires.

The calling itself is a real art and is learned only after a good deal of practice. Ideally, one using these dances should visit some square dances in order to get the spirit of them and to learn how they are called. The call for each figure should be made just before the beginning of a phrase of music so that the dancers will begin the figure with the phrase. If there are several sets of dancers the caller watches one set to guide him in timing his calls, and is prompt to call the next change in figure before the dancers finish the one which they are executing.

In writing the descriptions of these dances I have indicated the number of counts which each movement takes merely as an aid to one who is working out the dance for the first time. The dancers should not be made "count-conscious" but should be taught to listen for the call and to the music. It is customary to play eight measures of music before each new change to set the rhythm for the dancers and to give the caller an opportunity to start his call properly.

The step used throughout the dancing is a rather fast gliding movement between a walking and a running step. For the women this almost never varies. Among the more experienced dancers, one often sees the men execute intricate, spontaneous, and original foot patterns which are very picturesque to watch.

The square dance is danced in a set of eight, with four couples facing a square, as indicated by the following diagram. I have numbered the couples I, II, III, and IV, counter-clockwise around the set. Couples I and III are called head couples, or head and foot couples; and II and IV are called side couples.

To begin a dance it is customary for Couple I to lead up to Couple II. Many times the caller will call "the first two couples lead up to the right" meaning that Couples III and IV will execute the same figure which I and II do, simultaneously.

Again it makes an interesting dance to call "second couple follow up" after Couple I has passed Couple III, so that Couple II will be dancing with Couple III while Couple I is dancing with Couple IV. This continues with each successive couple "following up" after the preceding couple has passed two others. Each couple dances with each succeeding couple once around the set.

In some parts of the country the square dances begin and finish in a large circle of all the sets of dancers. Then as the figures are called, Couple I, or sometimes Couples I and III, lead out in each group of eight people and dance with the next couple on their right.

I would emphasize the fact again that the dances and calls vary in different parts of the country, and I suggest that each person working with these dances familiarize himself with the particular ways they are done in their own communities.

MUSIC

I am listing several well-known tunes which may be used for Quadrilles. This type of music is better suited for piano use than the type used in earlier times when the violin carried the melody. Many tunes of similar type are available; these I mention are merely suggestions. When a certain piece of music particularly fits a call, I have indicated that as especially suitable; others may be used. In most communities there are capable "fiddlers" who play the music which has been popular in their own neighborhoods, and when they can be secured for playing, they add much color and fun to the occasion. The same is true for "callers." It is suggested that local versions of the dances and music be used whenever possible.

The music should be played in the tempo of the fast march. To give variety, it is well to have the accompanist shift from one dance tune to another throughout the dance.

A Tisket, A Tasket
Aunt Dinah's Quilting Party
Billy Boy
Buffalo Girls
Camptown Races
Captain Jinks
Carry Me Back to Old Virginny
Darling Nelly Gray
Dixie

Farmer in the Dell
Gold Mine in the Sky
Good-Night, Ladies
Hand Me Down My Walking Cane
Hinkey Dinkey Parley Voo
Irish Washerwoman
I Want a Girl
Jingle Bells
John Brown's Indians
Kingdom Coming
Li'l Liza Jane
Listen to the Mocking Bird
Little Brown Jug
Mulberry Bush
My Old Kentucky Home
Oh! Susanna
Old Dan Tucker
Old Folks at Home
Old Zip Coon, or, Turkey in the Straw
Oh! Dem Golden Slippers
Polly-Wolly-Doodle
Pop Goes the Weasel
Red River Valley
Red Wing
Reuben, Reuben
Rig-a-Jig
She'll Be Coming 'Round the Mountain
Short'nin' Bread
Skip to My Lou
Soldier's Joy
Some Folks Do
The Arkansas Traveler
The Bear Went Over the Mountain
The Campbells Are Coming

The King of the Cannibal Islands
The Old Gray Mare
There'll Be a Hot Time in the Old Town Tonight
There is a Tavern in a Town
They Cut Down the Old Pine Tree
Turkey in the Straw, or Old Zip Coon
Wait for the Wagon
Wearing of the Green
When Johnny Comes Marching Home
When You and I Were Young, Maggie
Yankee Doodle

Following are old tunes frequently used by "fiddlers" for both "square" dance and contra-dance accompaniment:

College Hornpipe
Devil's Dream
Durang's Hornpipe
Fisher's Hornpipe
Haste to the Wedding
Hull's Victory Hornpipe
Irish Washerwoman
Lannigan's Ball
McDonald's Reel
Miss McLeod's Reel
Money Musk
New Century Hornpipe
Off She Goes
Opera Reel
Rickett's Hornpipe
Rory O'More
Rustic Reel
Sir Roger de Coverly
Soldier's Joy

Speed the Plough
St. Patrick's Day
The Campbells Are Coming
The Tempest
The White Cockade
The Wind That Shakes the Barley
Top of Cork Road
Turkey in the Straw
Vinton's Hornpipe

The following are good collections of music for the contra-dances:

"Harding's Collection of Two Hundred Jigs, Reels, and Country Dances." Published by Maurice Richmond, Inc., New York.

"Robbins Collection of Two Hundred Jigs, Reels, and Country Dances." Published by Robbins Music Corporation, New York.

"Kerr's Collection of Reels, Strathspeys, and Country Dances." Published by J. S. Kerr, Glasgow, Scotland.

"Pioneer Collection, Old Time Dances." Published by Paull-Pioneer Music Co., New York.

If a phonograph is available the following records may be used:

For Quadrilles:	Victor Records Number
"Chillicothe," "Virginny Shore"	20638
"Oh! Susanna," "Arkansas Traveler"	20638
"St. Patrick's Day"	21616
"Turkey in the Straw"	22131
"Captain Jinks"	20639
	and
	22991

"Camptown Races" .... 24538 (song)
"Soldier's Joy" 20592
"Yankee Doodle" and "Dixie Melodies" 24178
"Old Zip Coon" 20592
"Pop Goes the Weasel" 20151
                                        and
                                        20447

For a March Quadrille:

"El Capitan" and "Washington Post" 20191

For Virginia Reel:

"Virginia Reels" 20447

For Hornpipe:

"Young America Hornpipe" 20592

For Sicilian Circle:

"Sicilian Circle" 20639
                                        and
                                        22991

For Money Musk:

"Money Musk Nos. 1 and 2" 20447

For Polka:

"Heel and Toe Polka" 19909

For Schottische:

"Schottische" 19907

For Varsovienne:

"Varsovienne" 19910

Decca Album, Number 18 contains records for Rye Waltz and Schottische. "Tuxedo" and "Trilby" from this album are fine for quadrilles.

Decca Album, Number 19, has records for schottisches, polkas, two-steps, and waltzes.

QUADRILLES

SOLDIER'S JOY

ARRANGED BY ROBERT T. BENFORD

QUADRILLE I

FIRST CHANGE

Formation—Quadrille

SUGGESTED MUSIC: "Soldier's Joy" or "Camptown Races"

CALL

"Honor your partner,
Corners the same.
Head couples right and left through,
Right and left back.
Promenade across,
Promenade back.
Change your ladies,
Change them back.
Promenade across,
Right and left back."

Partners honor each other, and all turn and salute corners at the beginning of each quadrille.

1

Couples I and III change positions with a half right
and left .... 8 counts
Return .... 8 counts

2

Couples I and III change positions with a promenade   8 counts
Return .... 8 counts

3

Couples I and III, ladies chain .... 16 counts

HONOR PARTNERS

4

Couples I and III change positions with a promenade   8 counts
Return with a right and left ....   8 counts

Allemande left and grand right and left.

Repeat the dance with Couples II and IV.

SECOND CHANGE

SUGGESTED MUSIC: "Golden Slippers," "Buffalo Girls," or "Top of Cork Road"

CALL

"First couple lead to the right
Take your lady by the wrist,
Around next lady with a grape vine twist;
Back to the center with a whoa-haw-gee,
And around the gent whom you did not see,
Circle four and lead to the next," etc.

1

Boy of Couple I takes his partner's left hand in his
    right, leads her to Couple II, then completely
    around girl of Couple II, passing outside ....   16 counts

"First couple lead up to the right
Take your lady by the wrist,
Around next lady with a grape vine twist."

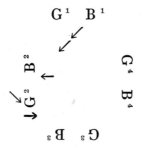

TOP OF CORK ROAD

ARRANGED BY ROBERT T. BENFORD

2

B[1] leads his partner to the center; makes a turn left;
then right; and leads back between G[2] and B[2],
completely around B[2] .... 16 counts

> "Back to the center with a whoa-haw-gee,
> And around the gent whom you did not see."

3

Couples I and II join hands and circle once left, and B[1] leads
the three to Couple III.

> "Circle four and lead to the next."

4

Repeat the "grape vine twist" with Couple III.

5

Finishing the twist, Couples I, II, and III join hands and circle
once left and lead to Couple IV.

> "Circle six and lead to the next."

6

Repeat the twist with Couple IV, finishing with the eight
circling once left to places.

7

> Allemande left and a grand right and left.
> All promenade around circle once.

Repeat all three times, each couple leading in turn, as:

> "Second couple lead to right
> Take your lady by the wrist," etc.

GRAPE VINE TWIST

THE BEAR WENT OVER THE MOUNTAIN

ARRANGED BY ROBERT T. BENFORD

JIG

SUGGESTED MUSIC: "Red Wing" or "The Bear Went Over the Mountain"

CALL

"All join hands and circle to the left.
Ladies balance to the right and swing.
Again to the right and swing.
Again to the right and swing.
Again to the right and swing partners.
Allemande left."

1

The four couples join hands and circle left .... 16 counts

2

Four girls lead to the right and swing with the boy
of the next couple .... 16 counts
Repeat on around the set finishing by swinging with
own partners .... 48 counts

3

Repeat 1 .... 16 counts

4

The four boys lead to the right and swing with the
girl of the next couple .... 16 counts
Repeat around the set .... 48 counts

Allemande left and promenade away.

QUADRILLE II

First Change

SUGGESTED MUSIC: "Animal Fair"

Formation—Quadrille

CALL

"Honor partners,
Corners the same.
Head couples right and left across.
Side couples right and left across.
Head couples right and left back.
Side couples right and left back.
Heads balance across.
Sides balance across.
Heads balance back.
Sides balance back.
Heads—ladies chain across.
Sides—ladies chain across.
Heads—ladies chain to place.
Sides—ladies chain to place.
Heads balance across.
Sides balance across.
Heads right and left back.
Sides right and left back.
Allemande left.
Right hands to partner and a grand right and left."

1

Couples I and III change positions with a half right
and left .... 8 counts
Couples II and IV, the same .... 8 counts

43

2

Couples I and III return to place with a half right
    and left .... 8 counts
Couples II and IV, the same .... 8 counts

3

Couples I and III change positions with a balance four 8 counts
Couples II and IV, the same .... 8 counts

4

Couples I and III return to place with a balance four . 8 counts
Couples II and IV, the same .... 8 counts

5

Couples I and III change ladies .... 8 counts
Couples II and IV, the same .... 8 counts

6

Couples I and III, change ladies to place .... 8 counts
Couples II and IV, the same .... 8 counts

7

Couples I and III change positions with a balance four 8 counts
Couples II and IV, the same .... 8 counts

8

Couples I and III return to positions with a half right
    and left .... 8 counts
Couples II and IV, the same .... 8 counts

Allemande left and grand right and left.

SECOND CHANGE

SUGGESTED MUSIC: "Oh! Susanna"

CALL

"Head couple forward and back,
Forward again and form a line of four.
Head couples forward and back,
Forward again and hold.
Side four right and left.
Balance four.
Ladies chain.
Promenade across.
Right and left back.
Heads circle four.
Right and left to place."

BALANCE FOUR

1

Couple I forward and back .... 8 counts
Forward again and form a line of four with Couple III,
    facing the head of the set .... 8 counts

Head

B^2 G_4

G^2 B_4

B_1 G_3 B_3 G_1

2

Couples I and III advance in a line forward and back 8 counts
Forward again and hold in the center of the set ..... 8 counts

Head

B^2 G_4

G^2 B_1 G_3 B_3 G_1 B_4

3

Couples II and IV right and left .... 16 counts

$B^2 \rightarrow$ $\leftarrow G_4$

$G^2 \rightarrow$ B_1 G_3 B_3 G_1 $\leftarrow B_4$

4

Couples II and IV balance across and back .... 16 counts
   (Couple IV balances across, passing in front of the line of
four, and back behind it. Couple II balances across behind the
line and back in front of it.)

5

Couples II and IV, ladies chain .... 16 counts
  (Girl of Couple IV crossing in front of the line, returning behind; girl of Couple II crossing behind, returning in front.)

6

Couples II and IV balance across and right and left
  back .... 16 counts

7

Couples I and III join hands and circle once left, then
  Right and left to original places .... 16 counts
                    Allemande left.
  Repeat the dance with the side couples forming the line.

JIG

SUGGESTED MUSIC: "Rig-a-Jig" or "Captain Jinks"

CALL

*"All join hands and circle to the left.
Heads balance across and back.
Sides the same.
All swing partners and promenade away."*

1

All join hands and circle to the left .... 16 counts

2

Couples I and III balance across and back .... 16 counts

3

Couples II and IV balance across and back .... 16 counts

4

All swing partners and promenade away.

QUADRILLE III

Music same as for Quadrille I

FIRST CHANGE—Same as First Change of Quadrille I

SECOND CHANGE

SUGGESTED MUSIC: "When Johnny Comes Marching Home" or "Hand Me Down My Walking Cane"

CALL

"First couple lead to the right.
Circle four.
Leave your lady and lead to the next.
Circle three.
Take that lady and lead to the next.
Circle four.
Leave that lady and lead away home.
Head gents forward and back.
Forward again with a do-si-do.
Side six forward and back.
Do it again with the right hand over and the
    left hand under," etc.

1

Couple I leads to Couple II. They join hands and circle once left . . . . 8 counts

2

Boy of Couple I leaves his partner and advances to Couple III, where the three join hands and circle left . . . . 8 counts

SIX ON A SIDE

THE RIGHT HAND OVER AND THE LEFT HAND UNDER

3

Boy of Couple I now takes girl of Couple III with him
to Couple IV, where the four circle left .... 8 counts

4

Leaving girl of Couple III, the boy leads to his original
position .... 8 counts

B^1

G^1 B^2 G^2 G^4 B^4 G^3

B^3

5

B^1 and B^3 forward and back .... 8 counts

6

B^1 and B^3 do-si-do .... 8 counts

7

Side six forward and back .... 8 counts

8

The six advance again and B^2 turns G^2 to B^1 and G^1 to B^3,
G^1 passing under the raised arms of B^2 and G^2.
B^4 does likewise, passing G^3 to B^1, and G^4 to B^3 ... 8 counts

G^2 B^1 G^3

B^2 B^4

G^4 B^3 G^1

9

B ² and B ⁴ repeat as 5 and 6 above . . . . 16 counts

10

B ¹ and B ³ repeat as in 7 and 8 above . . . . 16 counts

B ¹

$$G^4 \; B^2 \; G^3 \qquad\qquad G^2 \; B^4 \; G^1$$

B ³

Figures 5, 6, 7, 8, repeat two more times; the last time each boy turns his own partner to place.

Allemande left.

Grand right and left with elbow swing.

JIG

SUGGESTED MUSIC: "Turkey in the Straw" or "She'll Be Coming 'Round the Mountain"

CALL

"All join hands and forward and back.
Swing on the corner.
Swing partners all.
Swing corner lady and promenade the hall."

1

Join hands in circle of eight and forward and back . . .   8 counts

THE GIRL I LEFT BEHIND ME

ARRANGED BY ROBERT T. BENFORD

2
Each boy swings the girl at his left . . . .   8 counts

3
Each swings his own partner . . . .   8 counts

4
Each swings left-hand girl again and she becomes his
   new partner . . . .   8 counts

5
All promenade once around the set . . . .   16 counts

The dance repeats until each boy promenades with his original
partner.

QUADRILLE IV

FIRST CHANGE—Same as First Change of Quadrille I

SECOND CHANGE

SUGGESTED MUSIC: "The Girl I Left Behind Me"

CALLER'S SONG

"First couple lead up to the right,
Balance there so kindly,
Pass right through and balance two,
And swing with the girl behind you.
Take that lady and lead to the next,
Balance there so kindly,
Pass right through, and balance two,
And swing with the girl behind you."

The caller usually sings this to the tune "The Girl I Left Behind Me." For that reason I have called it "Caller's Song."

1

Couple I lead to Couple II and balance . . . .   8 counts

> "First couple lead up to the right,
> Balance there so kindly."

2

Couple I passes through Couple II, couples finishing
back to back . . . .   4 counts

> "Pass right through and balance two."

Boy of Couple I turns and swings girl of Couple II,
while boy of Couple II and girl of Couple I swing . .   4 counts

> "And swing with the girl behind you."

Boy of Couple I continues on around the set, taking a new lady at each couple until he reaches his original place.

Finish with an allemande left, and a grand right
and left . . . .   32 counts

The dance repeats, boy of Couple II progressing on around the set, taking a new lady at each couple until he reaches his original place.

The dance continues until each boy has completed the circuit. Finish with an allemande left, and a grand right and left.

JIG

SUGGESTED MUSIC: "Captain Jinks"

1

Partners stand in position . . . .   8 counts

> "I'm Captain Jinks on the Horse Marines,
> I feed my horse on corn and beans,"

CAPTAIN JINKS

ARRANGED BY ROBERT T. BENFORD

Partners face each other and bow .... 4 counts
  "Salute your partner if you're not green"

Stand in position .... 4 counts
  "For that's the style in the army."

2

Join hands in circle of eight and move left, walking
  steps .... 16 counts
      "All join hands and circle to the left,
      Circle to the left, circle to the left,
      All join hands and circle to the left
      For that's the style in the army."

3

Partners stand in position .... 4 counts
  "Captain Jinks got tight last night."

Boys pass to lady of the couple at the right .... 4 counts
  "The gentleman passes to the right."

Boys swing new partners .... 8 counts
      "Then swing your lady with all your might
      For that's the style in the army."

Repeat from beginning until boys have reached original places.

THE HEAD TWO GENTS CROSS OVER

ARRANGED BY ROBERT T. BENFORD

QUADRILLE V

Formation—Quadrille

SUGGESTED MUSIC: "Good-Night, Ladies"

CALL

"First four forward and pay address.
Turn to the right and address.
Turn to the left and address.
Back to place and address partners.
Allemande left."

1

Couples I and III forward and salute .... 8 counts

2

Couples I and III turn to face the couple at their right
and salute .... 8 counts

3

Couples I and III turn to the couple at their left and
salute .... 8 counts

4

Couples I and III back to place and all salute partners   8 counts
Allemande left and a grand right and left.

THE HEAD TWO GENTS CROSS OVER

SECOND CHANGE

CALLER'S SONG

"The head two gents cross over and by the opposite stand.
The side two gents cross over and all join hands.
Honors on the corners,
Salute your partners all,
Swing with the corner lady, and promenade the hall."

1

Boys of Couples I and III change places .... 8 counts

"The head two gents cross over and by the opposite stand."

Boys of Couples II and IV change places .... 4 counts
      "The side two gents cross over"

Join hands in circle of eight .... 4 counts
      "And all join hands."

Boys turn and salute the girl at the left .... 4 counts
      "Honors on the corner."

All salute partners .... 4 counts
      "Salute your partners all."

Boys swing with the girl at the left .... 4 counts
      "Swing with the corner lady,"

Finishing the swing with the corner lady, the boy
    takes her hand on his arm ready for a promenade .. 4 counts
      "And promenade the hall."

2

All promenade once around the set .... 16 counts

Repeat the dance until boys promenade with original partners.

JIG

SUGGESTED MUSIC: "Buffalo Girls" or "Dixie"

CALLER'S SONG

1. *"Head two couples on the inside 'round*
   Inside 'round, inside 'round.
   Head two couples on the inside 'round
   And balance to your places."

ALL PROMENADE

2. *"Swing your partners 'round and 'round*
   'Round and 'round, 'round and 'round
   Swing your partners 'round and 'round
   And balance to your places."

3. *"Star on the corner with a right hand cross*
   Right hand cross, right hand cross
   Star on the corner with a left hand cross
   And balance to your places."

4. *"All   promenade to a hoppin up and down*
   Hopping up and down, hopping up and down
   All promenade to a hopping up and down
   And balance to your places."

1

Couples I and III two-step around the inside of the
set and back to places .... 16 counts

2

Couples I and III swing partners in the center of the
set moving back into places on last four counts.. 16 counts

3

Couples I and III perform a star with the right hands
with Couples II and IV respectively, changing with
the call to star with the left hands .... 16 counts

4

All couples promenade once around the set .... 16 counts

The dance repeats with the side two couples leading. During
the last figure the dancers promenade away.

QUADRILLE VI

First Change

Music same as for Quadrille I

CALL

*"Heads right and left
Balance and turn partners
Ladies chain, and promenade."*

1

Couples I and III, right and left .... 16 counts

2

Couples I and III, balance to partners and swing.... 16 counts

3

Couples I and III, ladies chain .... 16 counts

4

All couples promenade once around the set .... 16 counts
Repeat all with side couples leading.

SECOND CHANGE

SUGGESTED MUSIC: "Oh! Susanna" or "Listen to the Mocking
Bird"

CALL

"First couple lead up to the right
Make a star with an eight-hand cross.
Ladies bow, gents know how,
Hold your holds and get there now.
Circle four.
Right and left through and lead to the next."

1

Couple I leads to Couple II. Girls clasp both hands. Boys
clasp both hands over the joined hands of the girls .. 8 counts

> "First couple lead up to the right.
> Make a star with an eight-hand cross."

2

Boys, keeping hands joined, swing arms over the girls'
heads and encircle them .... 4 counts
Girls do likewise with boys .... 4 counts

> "Ladies bow, gents know how,
> Hold your holds and get there now."

THE SUGAR BOWL

3

In this formation, the group circles left with sliding
steps .... 8 counts

4

Couples I and II join hands and circle half left...... 4 counts
Couple I right and left half with Couple II and lead
to Couple III .... 4 counts
Couple I repeats the dance with Couples III and IV, as with II.
When Couple I reaches original place, all allemande
left .... 8 counts
Grand right and left .... 16 counts
The whole figure is repeated until Couples II and III and IV
have also been entirely around the set.

This change is sometimes called the "sugar bowl"; sometimes
the "basket quadrille."

JIG

SUGGESTED MUSIC: "Red River Valley"

CALL

"All join hands and circle to the left.
Ladies in the center with a right hand star,
Circle half and swing the gentleman there.
Ladies in the center with a left-hand star,
Circle half and swing where you are."

1

All join hands and circle once left .... 16 counts

2

The four girls form a star in the center with right
hands and circle half around .... 8 counts
Each girl now swings with boy opposite her partner.. 8 counts

3

Girls form a star with left hands and circle half around   8 counts
Girls swing partners ....   8 counts
Allemande left, and swing partners ....   16 counts
  Repeat all, the boys forming the star in the center.

EXTRA FIRST CHANGES

FIRST CHANGE 1

MUSIC SUGGESTED: "Reuben, Reuben"

CALL

"First couple leads to the right,
  Go round that couple and swing as you meet.
  Back in the center and swing both feet.
  Circle four.
  Right and left and lead to the next."

1

Couple I leads to Couple II, passes around this couple,
  boy going to the left and the girl to the right.....   8 counts
B^1 and G^1 swing behind Couple II ....   8 counts

  "First couple leads up to the right,
    Go round that couple and swing as you meet."

2

B^1 and G^1 return by opposite paths to the center of
  the set where they swing again ....   16 counts

  "Back in the center and swing both feet."

3

Couples I and II join hands and circle left . . . .   8 counts
Right and left, Couple I leading on to Couple III . . . .   8 counts

> "Circle four,
> Right and left and lead to the next."

The figures 1, 2, 3 are repeated with Couples III and IV.

4

When Couple I reaches original position, an allemande
left and a grand right and left are called . . . .   24 counts

5

All swing partners . . . .   8 counts
     The complete figure is repeated with Couples II, III, and IV
leading in turn.
     If desired, Couple III may do the change with Couple IV
while Couple I is doing it with Couple II. This makes a more
interesting pattern and hastens the figure. The only change in
the call at the beginning would be "Head couples lead to the
right, etc."

First Change 2

MUSIC SUGGESTED: "Gold Mine in the Sky" or "Camptown
Races"

CALL

> *"First couple right and left with the right-hand couple.*
> *Balance four with the left-hand couple.*
> *Ladies chain with the opposite couple.*
> *Allemande left and a grand right and left."*

1

Couples I and II right and left .... 16 counts

"Right and left with the right-hand couple."

2

Couples I and IV balance four .... 16 counts

"Balance four with the left-hand couple."

3

Couples I and III ladies chain .... 16 counts

"Ladies chain with the opposite couple."

4

Allemande left and a grand right and left .... 24 counts

Swing partners all .... 8 counts

If desirable, instead of swinging partners, dancers may
   two-step once around the set and back to places... 32 counts

   Repeat all three times with Couples II, III, and IV leading in
turn.

First Change 3

MUSIC SUGGESTED: "Oh! Dem Golden Slippers"

CALL

"A grand right and left.
Ladies star with the right hand half way 'round;
Back with the left hand, hopping up and down.
Partners with the right hand all the way 'round;
Back with the left hand, I'll be bound.
All promenade."

1

Partners face, grand right and left . . . . 16 counts

2

Girls advance to the center of set, give right hands in
    star formation, and circle half . . . . 8 counts

"Star with the right hand, half way 'round."

3

Reverse direction, left hands joined . . . . 8 counts

"Back with the left hand, hopping up and down."

4

Partners take right hands and swing once around . . . . 8 counts

"Partners with the right hand all the way 'round."

Back with left hands . . . . 8 counts

"Back with the left hand, I'll be bound."

5

Partners join hands and promenade around the set
    and back to places . . . . 16 counts
(Sometimes dancers two-step around the set instead
    of the ordinary "promenade" . . . . 32 counts)

EXTRA SECOND CHANGES

Second Change 1

SUGGESTED MUSIC: "The Wearing of the Green" or "I Want a
    Girl"

CALL

"Head couples lead to the right,
Change partners and chassé out.
Right and left.
Balance four.
Ladies chain.
Balance across and chassé by one couple.
Forward four and back.
Forward and swing partners to place."

1

Couples I and III lead to II and IV respectively..... 8 counts

2

Couples I and II and Couples III and IV change partners, and each boy leads his new partner to the following position .... 8 counts

Head

G^1 B^2 G^4 B^3

B^1 G^2 B^4 G^3

3

B^1 and G^2 do a complete right and left with B^2
and G^1,

—while .... 16 counts

B^3 and G^4 do the same with B^4 and G^3.

4

B^2 and G^1 balance across and back with B^1 and G^2,

—while .... 16 counts

B^3 and G^4 do the same with B^4 and G^3.

5

Same couples as above, ladies chain . . . . 16 counts

6

B ^{2} and G ^{1}, and B ^{1} and G ^{2} change sides with a balance
                   —while . . . . 8 counts
B ^{3} and G ^{4}, and B ^{4} and G ^{3} do the same.

G ^{2} B ^{1} G ^{3} B ^{4}

B ^{2} G ^{1} B ^{3} G ^{4}

B ^{1} and G ^{2} chassé by G ^{3} and B ^{4}.
                   —while . . . . 8 counts
B ^{2} and G ^{1} chassé by B ^{3} and G ^{4}.

G ^{3} B ^{4} G ^{2} B ^{1}

B ^{3} G ^{4} B ^{2} G ^{1}

7

All forward and back . . . . 8 counts
Forward again, each boy takes his own partner and
  swings her to place . . . . 8 counts

8

All promenade around the set . . . . 16 counts

Second Change 2

SUGGESTED MUSIC: "Oh! Dem Golden Slippers"

"First couple lead to the right,
Two gents in the center with an elbow swing.
Opposite lady the same old thing.
Back in the center with an elbow swing.
Swing your partner with a pigeon wing.
Circle half, and right and left to the next," etc.

1

Couple I leads to Couple II .... 8 counts

2

Boys hook elbows and swing once around .... 8 counts

3

Each boy now hooks left elbow with the opposite girl
and swings her once around .... 8 counts

4

Repeat 2 .... 8 counts

5

Each boy swings his own partner with left elbow... 8 counts

6

Couples I and II join hands and circle half around,
then right and left half, Couple I leading on to the
next couple .... 8 counts
Repeat with each couple.
Finish with:
    Grand right and left with the elbow swing.

ELBOW SWING

Second Change 3

suggested music: "The Farmer in the Dell"

1

Couple I forward and back . . . . 8 counts
Forward again and circle half with Couple III . . . . . . 8 counts

2

Couple I right and left half with Couple III . . . . 8 counts
Girl of Couple I passes to her right to join hands with
  Couple II while boy of Couple I goes to join with
  Couple IV . . . . 8 counts

3

The two groups of three do-si-do, circling as they do so 16 counts

$$G^2 \quad B^2 \quad \quad \quad G^4 \quad B^4$$
$$G^1 \rightarrow \quad \leftarrow B^1$$

$$G^3 \quad B^3$$

4

Boy and girl of Couple I leave the side couples and
  circle half with Couple III . . . . 8 counts
Couple I right and left half with Couple III . . . . 8 counts
Girl of Couple I passes to Couple IV and the boy to
  Couple II . . . . 8 counts

5

Side threes do-si-do . . . . 16 counts

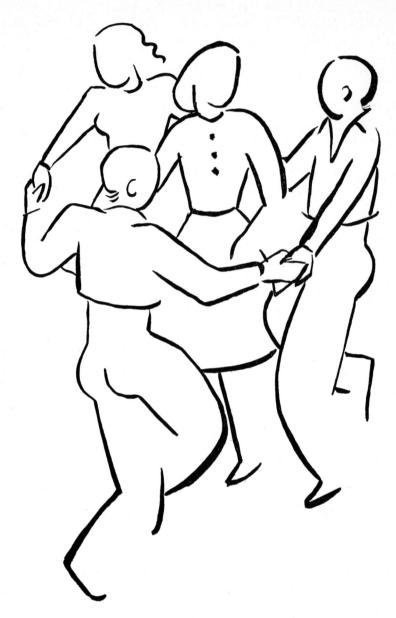

BIRDIE IN THE CENTER

6

Boy and girl of Couple I leave side couples, circle half
  with Couple III, and right and left to place ...... 16 counts
Allemande left and swing partners .... 16 counts

    Repeat the dance with each couple as leading.

SECOND CHANGE 4

SUGGESTED MUSIC: "Rig-a-Jig"

CALL

"First couple leads up to the right.
Birdie in the center and three hands round.
Birdie fly out and Hawkey fly in.
Hawkey fly out and give Birdie a swing.
Circle four.
Right and left through and lead to the next."

1

Couple I lead to Couple II .... 8 counts

    "First couple lead up to the right."

2

Couple II and boy of Couple I join hands and circle
  once left around girl of Couple I .... 8 counts

    "Birdie in the center and three hands round."

3

Boy of Couple I changes places with his partner. The
  three circle left .... 8 counts

    "Birdie fly out and Hawkey fly in."

4

Boys of Couples I and II swing their partners ......   8 counts

    "Hawkey fly out and give Birdie a swing."

5

Couples I and II join hands and circle half left; then
    half right and left, Couple I passing on to Couple III.   8 counts
The dance repeats until Couple I has reached original place.
Finish with:
    Allemande left and a grand right and left.

SECOND CHANGE 5

SUGGESTED MUSIC: "Little Brown Jug"

CALL

"First couple lead up to the right.
Chassé right behind that couple,
With the right hand across
And the left hand back,
Chassé back the same old track.
Promenade down the center and back.
Circle four.
Right and left to the next."

1

Couple I leads to Couple II ....   8 counts

    "First couple lead up to the right."

2

Couple I separates, the boy going to his left and the girl to her right, around Couple II . . . . 8 counts

"Chassé right behind that couple."

3

Taking right hands they pass each other, turn and pass back, taking left hands . . . . 8 counts

"With the right hand across
And the left hand back."

4

Boy and girl chassé to meet each other again in front of Couple II . . . . 8 counts

"Chassé back the same old track."

5

Couple I join hands and promenade down and back between girl and boy of Couple II . . . . 8 counts

"Promenade down the center and back."

6

Couple I and II circle half left . . . . 4 counts

Then

Half right and left, Couple I passing on to Couple III 4 counts

Repeat the above until Couple I has reached original position.

Finish with:
Allemande left, and grand right and left.

SECOND CHANGE 6

SUGGESTED MUSIC: "Li'l Liza Jane"

CALL

"First lady swing right-hand man with the right hand around.
Partner with the left hand, left hand around.
Lady in the center and seven hands around.
Lady swing partner and everybody swing."

1

Girl of Couple I faces boy of Couple II, takes his right
hand in hers and turns him once around .... 8 counts
She now gives her left hand to her own partner and
turns him once around .... 8 counts

2

Girl of Couple I steps into the center of the set and the
other seven circle to the left .... 16 counts

3

Girl of Couple I swings with her partner, and all couples swing .... 16 counts

4

All promenade once around the set .... 16 counts

Repeat three times, the girl of the next couple leading each
time.

Finish with:
    Allemande left.
    Right hand to partner and left hand to next.
    Reverse and give right hand to partner, and allemande left.

SECOND CHANGE 7

SUGGESTED MUSIC: "There'll Be a Hot Time in the Old Town Tonight"

CALL

"First couple lead up to the right.
Dos-a-balinet and gents contra-dance.
Break with the right and swing with the left.
Then break with the right and swing with the left.
Circle four hands left
And right and left and lead to the next."

1

Couple I leads to Couple II and the two girls change places and balance. This leaves the girls facing outward and the boys facing inward in a circle of four, hands joined .... 8 counts

"First couple lead up to the right.
Dos-a-balinet and gents contra-dance."

2

Each boy now drops hands with the girl on his right and turns the girl on his left half around, finishing with the boys facing outward and the girls facing inward. Balance .... 8 counts

"Break with the right and swing with the left."

3

Each boy again drops hands with the girl on the right and turns the girl on his left completely around so that all face inward in a circle of four .... 8 counts

"Then break with the right and swing with the left."

DOS-A-BALINET

4

The four circle half left, and right and left on to Couple III.

"Circle four. Right and left and lead to the next."

Couple I repeat the dance with Couples III and IV.

The pattern of this dance is very attractive if the second, third, and fourth couples "follow up" as described in the discussion of "Quadrilles or Square Dances" on page 19.

SECOND CHANGE 8

SUGGESTED MUSIC: "Skip to My Lou" or "Cannibal Islands"

CALL

"First couple leads up to the right.
Lady go 'round and gent cut through.
Gent go 'round and lady cut through.
Circle four and lead to the next."

Sometimes called:

"Chase the squirrel around the two,
The lady goes 'round and the gent cut through.
Back around the same old track,
The gent goes 'round and the lady cuts back."

1

Couple I leads to Couple II, G^1 going around outside B^2, B^1 following. G^1 continues on around G^2, B^1 cuts through between B^2 and G^2.

THE KING OF THE CANNIBAL ISLANDS

ARRANGED BY ROBERT T. BENFORD

LADY GO 'ROUND AND GENT CUT THROUGH

B¹ now leads around outside B², G¹ following. B¹
    continues on around G², G¹ cutting through be-
    tween B² and G²
(This brings Couple I to a position facing Couple II) 16 counts

$$G^1 \quad B^1$$
$$\downarrow \quad \downarrow$$
$$B^2 \quad G^2$$

2

Couples I and II join hands and circle half left. Then
    they right and left, Couple I leading on to Couple III 16 counts
Couple I repeats the figure with Couples III and IV.

The dance repeats until all couples have also completed the circuit.

Finish with:
Allemande left and grand right and left.

SECOND CHANGE 9

SUGGESTED MUSIC: Same as for Second Change 8

CALL

"First couple leads up to the right;
Lady around lady and gent go slow.
Lady around gent and gent don't go.
Circle four and lead to the next," etc.

1

Couple I leads to Couple II. G^1 followed by B^1, leads around G^2, passing between G^2 and B^2 .... 16 counts

2

G^1 now goes around B^2, while B^1 stands in place in front of Couple II .... 16 counts

3

Couples I and II join hands and circle one-half, then right and left half, Couple I leading on to Couple III.
Repeat with each couple.
Repeat all, each couple leading in turn.
Finish with:
Allemande left and grand right and left.

SECOND CHANGE 10

SUGGESTED MUSIC: "They Cut Down the Old Pine Tree" or "Carry Me Back to Old Virginny"

CALL

"All join hands and circle to the left.
Head two couples lead to the right.
Circle four hands a half
And right and left eight.
Allemande left.
Grand right and left.
Half around with an elbow swing.
Swing partners and promenade back."

1

All circle left . . . . 16 counts

2

Couples I and III lead to the right and circle half with
Couples II and IV respectively . . . . 8 counts

3

The four couples now right and left the width of the
set, swinging into original places when they finish . . 32 counts
(If desired this right and left may be the width of the hall,
taking in other sets.)

B^1 → ← G_2 → B^4 → ← G_3

G^1 → ← B_2 G^4 → ← B_3

4

Allemande left

Grand right and left .... 24 counts

Repeat the above four figures with the side couples leading up to the right. If desired the right and left may be the whole length of the hall, with all other sets which are in line.

SECOND CHANGE 11

SUGGESTED MUSIC: "When You and I Were Young, Maggie"

CALL

*"First couple around the set.
Right and left with the couple they meet.
Ladies chain.
Balance four.
Allemande left.
Swing partners to place."*

1

Couple I promenades around the outside of the set... 16 counts

2

Couple I right and left with Couple II

                —while .... 16 counts

Couple III and IV do likewise.

3

Couples I and II, ladies chain

                —while .... 16 counts

Couples III and IV, ladies chain.

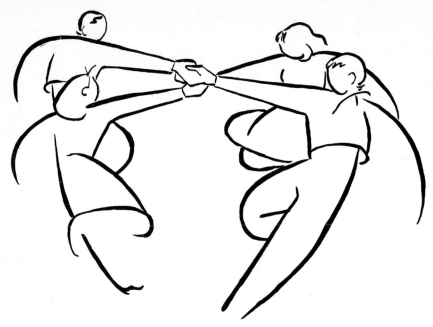

STAR WITH RIGHT HAND CROSS

4

Couples **I** and **II**, balance across and back
     —while .... 16 counts
Couples **III** and **IV**, balance across and back.

5

Allemande left and swing partners to place .... 16 counts
 Repeat all, with each successive couple around the outside, etc.

SECOND CHANGE 12

SUGGESTED MUSIC: "Oh! Dem Golden Slippers"

CALL

"First couple lead to the right.
Form a star with the right hand across.
Left hand back and don't get lost.
Circle four and right and left six.
Lead to the next," etc.

DUCK AND DIVE

1

Couple I leads to Couple II, form a right-hand star
  and circle once .... 16 counts
Reverse with a left-hand star .... 8 counts
Circle four, half left, then right and left six.
(Couples I, II and IV the width of the set) .... 32 counts

→
B¹   ← G²   ← G⁴

G¹→   ← B²   ← B⁴

G³ B³

2

Couples I and II circle half left, and right and left, Couple I
leading on to Couple III, where "1" is repeated. Instead of
"Right and Left Six" here, the call is "Duck and Dive" the
length of the hall. This is executed much as a "Right and Left"

the length of the hall, the difference being that partners join inside hands and pass under the raised hands of the couple whom they are facing, then raise hands for advancing couple to pass under, thus alternating under and over the length of the room. Couple I in each set goes "under" first. When a couple reaches the end of the room, the boy turns his partner about and they return over and under to place.

SECOND CHANGE 13

SUGGESTED MUSIC: "There is a Tavern in a Town" or "Jingle Bells"

CALL

"Two head ladies lead to the right.
Circle three hands 'round.
Head gents forward and back.
Forward again with a do-si-do.
Forward six and back.
Forward again and circle a half.
Lone gents forward and back.
Forward again and do-si-do.
Forward six and back.
Forward again and circle a half.
Lone gents lead to the right.
Circle four and right and left eight.
Allemande left and swing partners."

1

G¹ leads to Couple II while G³ leads to Couple IV, and the two groups of three circle once left, finishing three in a line on the sides of the set . . . . 16 counts

"Two head ladies lead to the right.
Circle three hands 'round."

(This leaves B^1 and B^3 standing alone; G^1 standing
at the left of B^2; G^3 at the left of B^4.)
(See diagram describing 4 of Second Change, Quadrille III.)

2

B^1 and B^3 forward and back .... 8 counts

"Lone gents forward and back."

3

B^1 and B^3 do-si-do .... 8 counts

"Forward again with a do-si-do."

4

The two groups of three on the side forward and back   8 counts

"Forward six and back."

5

Threes advance again and make a half circle left
finishing in a line of three on the opposite sides of
the set .... 8 counts

"Forward again and circle a half."

6 and 7

Same as 2 and 3

"Lone gents forward and back.
Forward again with a do-si-do."

8 and 9

Same as 4 and 5. (This brings the threes back to
their first position in the set.)

10

B¹ leads to the three at his right, while B³ does likewise, and each group of four circles once to the left   8 counts

"Lone gents lead to the right. Circle four."

11

On finishing "circle four," the eight perform a right
and left across the set . . . . 32 counts

"And right and left eight."

12

Allemande left and swing partners . . . . 16 counts
When these figures are finished, repeat with G² and G⁴ leading.

When the eight right and left, they may do so with other sets
as suggested in Second Change 10.

SECOND CHANGE 14

Same music as for Second Change 13

CALL

"First two couples lead out to the right.
Circle four hands 'round.
Gents back to place.
Lone gents go forward and back.
Forward again with a do-si-do.
Side six right and left with the right-hand lady.

Balance four with the left-hand lady.
Ladies chain with the right-hand lady.
Half promenade and half right and left with the
    left-hand lady
Two lone gents lead to the right.
Circle four and right and left eight.
Allemande left and an allemande right.
Swing partners."

1

Couples I and III lead to Couples II and IV respectively and each four circles once left, after which the boys fall back to their own places .... 8 counts

(This leaves G^1 with Couple II and G^3 with Couple IV, as in Second Change 13.)

"First two couples lead out to the right.
Circle four hands 'round."

2

B^1 and B^3 forward and back .... 8 counts
"Lone gents go forward and back."

3

B^1 and B^3 do-si-do .... 8 counts
"Forward again with a do-si-do."

4

B^2 and B^4 take own partners and the four right and left .... 16 counts
(This leaves G^1 and G^3 standing alone.)

"Side six right and left with the right-hand lady."

5

B^2 and B^4 now take G^1 and G^3 respectively and balance across to each other's position and back ..... 16 counts

> "Balance four with the left-hand lady."

6

B^2 and G^2, B^4 and G^4 ladies chain .... 16 counts

> "Ladies chain with the right-hand lady."

7

B^2 and G^1 and B^4 and G^3 promenade across the set and right and left back .... 16 counts

> "Half promenade and half right and left with the left-hand lady."

8

B^1 and B^3 lead to the right and the four on each side of the set circle once left .... 8 counts

> "Two lone gents lead to the right. Circle four."

9

The eight right and left across the set and return to the positions they were in when they finished Figure 8 .... 32 counts

> "Right and left eight."

10

The two fours circle one-half and right and left to original places .... 8 counts

DIP FOR THE OYSTER

11

Allemande left .... 8 counts

12

Allemande right .... 8 counts

13

Swing partners .... 8 counts

Repeat the dance with the side two couples leading.

SECOND CHANGE 15

SUGGESTED MUSIC: "There is a Tavern in a Town" or "Buffalo Girls"

CALL

"All join hands and circle to the left.
Fall back in a single line,
Ladies in front and gents behind.
Swing partners, corner too.
Right and left all the way through.
First couple leads up to the right.
Dip for the oyster, dive for the clam,
Dive for the sardines
Get a whole can."

or

(*"Dip for the oyster, dive for the clam,*
Now take a dip for the promised land.")
"Circle four.
Opposite by the right.

Partner by the left.
Opposite by the right.
Half swing and half promenade,
And on to the next."

1

Join hands and circle to the left .... 8 counts

     "All join hands and circle to the left."

2

Circle to the right in file, ladies leading .... 8 counts

     "Fall back in a single line,
     Ladies in front and gents behind."

3

All boys turn partners once around with right hand,
    then turn girl at the left (as in allemande left) .... 8 counts

     "Swing partners, corner too."

4

Grand right and left .... 16 counts

     "Right and left all the way through."

5

Couple I leads to the right and joins hands with
    Couple II .... 4 counts
Couple II makes an arch and pulls Couple I between
    them under the arch .... 4 counts

     "Dip for the oyster."

Still holding hands Couple I backs into place .... 4 counts

6

Couple II now dips under the raised hands of Couple
I, and back . . . .   8 counts

"Dive for the clam."

7

Couple I dips again under the raised hands of Couple
II and back . . . .   8 counts

"Dive for sardines, get a whole can."

8

Couples I and II circle four . . . .   4 counts

9

Each of the two boys turns the opposite girl once
around with the right hand . . . .   4 counts

"Opposite by the right."

10

Turn partners once around with the left hand . . . . . .   4 counts

"Partners by the left."

11

Turn opposites again with the right hand . . . .   4 counts

"Opposite by the right."

12

B[1] turns his partner with the left hand and the couple
leads on to Couple III. At the same time B[2] turns
his partner around with the left hand, to place . . . .   8 counts

ARKANSAS TRAVELER

ARRANGED BY ROBERT T. BENFORD

"Half swing and half promenade;
On to the next."

Couple I repeats the above with Couples III and IV. All of the dance is then repeated with each couple leading in turn.

SECOND CHANGE 16

SUGGESTED MUSIC: "Arkansas Traveler" or "Listen to the Mocking Bird"

CALL

"First lady and opposite gent forward and back.
Forward again and cross over.
Double chassé ladies in center, gents outside;
Then gents in the center and ladies outside.
Forward four and back.
Forward again and swing partners.
Allemande left.
Right hand to partners and grand right and left."

1

G^1 and B^3 forward and back . . . . 8 counts

"First lady and opposite gent forward and back."

2

The same two go forward again and exchange places . . 8 counts

"Forward again and cross over."

(This leaves the two girls in the position of Couple III and the boys in the position of Couple I.)

3

The two girls, facing each other, take both hands and chassé to the opposite side of the set, while the boys chassé across singly allowing the girls to pass between them .... 4 counts

Repeat, returning to places .... 4 counts

"Double chassé, ladies in the center, gents outside."

4

Repeat 3, boys passing between the two girls ...... 8 counts

"Then gents in the center and ladies outside."

5

The two boys and the two girls forward and back.... 8 counts

"Forward four and back."

6

Forward again and boys swing partners to place .... 8 counts

"Forward again and swing partners."

7

Allemande left and grand right and left .... 24 counts

8

Swing partners in place .... 8 counts

Repeat all with G^2 and B^4 leading.

Second Change 17

suggested music: "The Bear Went Over the Mountain"

CALL

"First couple up to the right.
Behind that couple and take a peek.
Back to the center, swing so neat.
Behind that couple, peek once more.
Back to the center, swing all four."

ALLEMANDE LEFT

TAKE A PEEK

1

Couple I leads to Couple II where they divide, the boy passing to the left of Couple II and the girl to the right. When they have passed, they peek at each other . . . . 8 counts

> "First couple up to the right.
> Behind that couple and take a peek."

2

B^1 and G^1 return by the same paths and swing in the center of the set . . . . 8 counts

> "Back to the center, swing so neat."

3

Repeat 1 . . . . 8 counts

> "Behind that couple, peek once more."

4

Repeat 2, and both couples swing . . . . 4 counts

> "Back to the center, swing all four."

5

Couples I and II circle four and right and left, Couple I leading on to Couple III . . . . 8 counts

Couple I repeats the figure with Couples III and IV. Finish with an allemande left and a grand right and left. The dance is then repeated with each successive couple leading.

RIGHT AND LEFT

SECOND CHANGE 18

TO THE TUNE OF "Darling Nelly Gray"

CALL

"The first man ltads his lady up to the right,
Where they circle to the left and they circle to the right.
They right and left through,
And they right and left back,
And he swings with his darling Nelly Gray.
Then he leads to the next
Where they balance there so fine;
And they circle to the left and they circle to the right.
They right and left through,
And they right and left back,
And he swings with his darling Nelly Gray.
Then they lead to the next where they balance there so fine,
And they circle to the left and they circle to the right, etc."

1

Couple I leads to Couple II. The four join hands and
circle left .... 4 counts
And right .... 4 counts

"The first man leads his lady up to the right,
Where they circle to the left and they circle to the right."

2

Couples I and II right and left .... 16 counts

"They right and left through,
And they right and left back."

TURKEY IN THE STRAW

ARRANGED BY ROBERT T. BENFORD

3

The two couples swing .... 4 counts

"And he swings with his darling Nelly Gray."

4

Couple I now advances to Couple III where the two
couples balance to each other .... 8 counts

"Then he leads to the next
Where they balance there so fine."

5

Couples I and III circle left and right .... 8 counts

"And they circle to the left and they circle to the right."

6

Repeat 2 .... 16 counts

"They right and left through,
And they right and left back."

7

Repeat 3 .... 4 counts

"And he swings with his darling Nelly Gray."

Couple I repeats the figure with Couple IV, after which an
allemande left and a grand right and left are called. The whole
dance is repeated with each successive couple leading.

SECOND CHANGE 19

SUGGESTED MUSIC: "Turkey in the Straw" or "Hot Time in the
Old Town Tonight"

CALL

"Join your hands and circle eight.
Fall back in a single line,
Ladies in the front and gents behind.
Swing partner, corner too.
Then right and left all the way through.
First couple out and circle four.
Drop that gent and circle three.
Shoot that pretty girl through to me.
Circle four.
Opposite by the right.
Partner by the left.
Opposite by the right.
Half swing and half promenade.
On to the next and circle four.
Drop that gent and circle three, etc."

1

All join hands and circle to the left . . . .   8 counts

"Join your hands and circle eight."

2

Circle to the right in file, ladies leading . . . .   8 counts

"Fall back in a single line,
Ladies in front and gents behind."

3

All boys turn partners once around with the right
hand, then turn girl at the left with the left hand . .   8 counts

"Swing partner, corner too."

4

Grand right and left .... 16 counts

"Right and left all the way through."

5

Couple I leads to Couple II and the four circle once
left .... 8 counts

"First couple out and circle four."

6

B^1 drops out and the three circle left .... 8 counts

"Drop that gent and circle three."

7

The three continue to circle left and when G^1 is opposite her partner, B^2 and G^2 pull her under their
raised arms to her partner, doing so with a snap .. 4 counts

"Shoot that pretty girl through to me."

8

Couples I and II circle left .... 4 counts

"Circle four."

9

Each of the two boys turns the opposite girl once
around with the right hand .... 4 counts

"Opposite by the right."

10

Turn partner once around with the left hand . . . .　4 counts

"Partners by the left."

11

Turn opposite again with the right hand . . . .　4 counts

"Opposite by the right."

12

B ^{1} turns his partner around with the left hand and leads on to Couple III. At the same time B ^{2} turns his partner around with the left hand to place . . . . .　8 counts

"Half swing and half promenade.
On to the next."

Couple I repeat the above with Couples III and IV. All of the dance is then repeated with each couple leading in turn.

Second Change 20

SUGGESTED MUSIC: "Oh! Dem Golden Slippers" or "Oh! Susanna"

"Listen to the music; listen to the call;
All join hands and waltz the hall.
Pat your foot and whirl on your heel.
Longer your dance, the better you feel.
First couple out, lady in the lead.
Gent fall through and take the lead.
Lady through the side door.
Meet your partners, swing four.
Circle four."

"Opposite by the right.
Partner by the left.
Opposite by the right.
Half swing and half promenade.
On to the next, lady in the lead, etc."

1

During the first two lines of the call the dancers join
hands and circle to the left . . . .   8 counts
On the next two lines of the call, they circle right . . .   8 counts

"Listen to the music; listen to the call;
All join hands and waltz the hall.
Pat your foot and whirl on your heel.
Longer you dance, the better you feel."

2

Couple I leads to Couple II, G^1 leading around to the
right of Couple II, boy following . . . .   8 counts

"First couple out, lady in the lead."

3

When B^1 reaches position between B^2 and G^2, he turns
toward the center of the set and takes the lead
around Couple II again, girl following . . . .   8 counts

"Gent falls through and takes the lead."

4

When the girl reaches the same place, she turns be-
tween B^2 and G^2 as did the boy . . . .   8 counts

"Lady through the side door."

5

Partners meet in front of Couple II, and both couples
  swing . . . .   8 counts

> "Meet your partners and swing four."

6

Two couples join hands and circle left . . . .   8 counts
> "Circle four."

7

Each boy now takes opposite girl by the right hand
  and turns her completely around . . . .   4 counts

> "Opposite by the right."

8

This puts all in position to turn own partners around
  by left hand . . . .   4 counts

> "Partner by the left."

9

Repeat 7 . . . .   4 counts
> "Opposite by the right."

10

B[1] turns partner again with the left hand and the couple moves
on to Couple III, as Couple II falls into own position.

> "Half swing and half promenade,
>   And on to the next."

Couple I repeats the above with Couples III and IV. On finishing with Couple IV, all do a grand right and left. All of the dance
is then repeated with each couple leading in turn.

EXTRA THIRD CHANGES

Jig Figure 1

SUGGESTED MUSIC: "Buffalo Girls"

CALL

"All join hands and circle to the left.
Circle to the right, ladies in the lead.
Ladies in the center back to back.
Gents around the outside track.
Salute your partners, and swing with the next," etc.

1

All circle left, hands joined .... 16 counts

2

All circle right, single file, girls leading .... 16 counts

3

Girls step into the center of the set facing outside
while boys circle in file around the set .... 16 counts

4

When boys reach own partners they salute, then
swing with the next girl .... 16 counts

Boys circle again, salute partners whom they have swung, and swing with the next. This continues until each boy swings with his original partner.

LADIES IN THE CENTER BACK TO BACK

The dance then repeats with the boys in the center.

Finish with:
 Allemande left.
 All promenade away.

Jig Figure 2

SUGGESTED MUSIC: "I Want a Girl"

CALL

"First couple up to the right.
Circle four hands round.
Lead to the next and circle six hands round.
Lead to the next and circle eight hands round.
Allemande left."

Couple I leads up to Couple II. They circle once left.. 16 counts
Couples I and II, keeping hands joined, advance to
 Couple III and circle six, once left .... 16 counts
Couples I, II, and III lead to Couple IV and all circle
 to the left .... 16 counts
 (This brings all back to original places.)
Allemande left and swing partners .... 16 counts
 Repeat until each couple has been the leader; then
 all promenade away.

Jig Figure 3

SUGGESTED MUSIC: "There'll be a Hot Time in the Old Town
 Tonight"
All join hands and circle to the left .... 16 counts
Same right .... 16 counts
Forward all and back .... 8 counts
Forward again and salute .... 8 counts
 All promenade away.

JIG FIGURE 4

"First couple lead to the right.
Swing with the opposite and swing her alone.
Swing with the one you call your own.
Swing with the opposite and don't be afraid.
Swing your partner and half promenade."

1

B^1 leads G^1 up to Couple II . . . .   8 counts
G^1 swings with B^2 and B^1 with G^2 . . . .   8 counts
B^1 swings with G^1 . . . .   8 counts
B^1 swings G^2, and B^2 with G^1 . . . .   8 counts
B^1 swings G^1 . . . .   8 counts
B^1 and G^1 promenade to Couple III.

2

Repeat 1 with Couples III and IV.
Repeat all, Couples II, III and IV making the circuit.
Finish with:
  All promenade.
The above call is sometimes called as follows:

"Swing your ma, swing your pa,
Don't forget Old Arkansaw."

or

"I'll swing your girl, you swing mine.
You swing your girl, I'll swing mine."

JIG FIGURE 5

SUGGESTED MUSIC: "Captain Jinks"

CALL

"Allemande left with the corners all.
Allemande right with your partners all.
Do-si-do with the corners all."

DO-SI-DO

"Do-si-do with partners all.
Everybody swing.
Allemande left and a grand right and left.
Forward all and promenade away."

DO-SI-DO

ARRANGED BY ROBERT T. BENFORD

1
All allemande left .... 4 counts

2
Turn partners with right hands .... 4 counts

3
Do-si-do with the corner person .... 4 counts

4
Do-si-do with partners .... 4 counts

5
All swing partners .... 4 counts

6
Allemande left .... 4 counts

7
Grand right and left .... 16 counts

8
All join hands and go forward and back .... 8 counts

All two-step as long as desired, or until the music stops.

JIG FIGURE 6

CALL

"Do-si-do with the corner lady.
Do-si-do with partners all.
Swing the corner lady,
And promenade the hall."

1

Each boy turns to the girl on his left and does a
do-si-do with her .... 4 counts

"Do-si-do with the corner lady."

2

All face partners and do-si-do .... 4 counts

"Do-si-do with partners all."

3

Each boy swings the girl at his left .... 8 counts

"Swing the corner lady."

4

Keeping new partners, all promenade once around the
set to the boys' places .... 16 counts

"And promenade the hall."

Repeat three times, finishing with a promenade away with
original partners.

Jig Figure 7

SUGGESTED MUSIC: "Red Wing" or "Wait for the Wagon"

CALL

"Head couple out and swing in the center.
And six hands 'round.
Allemande left and a grand right and left.
Promenade with partners."

1

While Couple I swings in the center of the set, the
remaining couples circle once to the left . . . . 16 counts

"Head couple out and swing in the center.
And six hands 'round."

2

Allemande left and a grand right and left . . . . 16 counts

3

All promenade around the set with a two-step . . . . . . 32 counts
Repeat all with Couples II, III, and IV swinging in turn in
the center.
On finishing the last figure, partners promenade away to seats.

Jig Figure 8

SUGGESTED MUSIC: "When You and I Were Young, Maggie" or
"There'll Be a Hot Time in the Old Town
Tonight"

CALL

"First couple lead up to the right.
Two ladies whirl.
Two gents whirl.
All four whirl and lead to the next."

1

Couple I leads to Couple II and the two girls turn once
around, singly .... 8 counts
Boys turn once around .... 4 counts
All four turn once around, singly .... 4 counts

2

Couples I and II join hands and circle half left, and
half right and left leading on to Couple III ...... 16 counts
Repeat with Couples III and IV.

Repeat the whole dance with Couples II, III, and IV, leading
in turn.

(If desired Couple III may start off at the same time Couple I
does. This makes the dance more interesting.)

JIG FIGURE 9

SUGGESTED MUSIC: "Red Wing" or "Reuben, Reuben"

CALL

"First lady lead up to the right.
Right hand 'round with the right-hand gent.
Left hand 'round with the partner.
Lady in the center and seven hands 'round.
Lady step out and gent step in.
Gent step out and give lady a swing."

(The last three lines are sometimes called as follows:

"Birdie in the center and seven hands 'round.
Birdie fly out and crow fly in.
Crow fly out and give birdie a swing.")

1

G^1 leads to Couple II where she joins right hands with
B^2 and turns once around with him .... 8 counts

"Right hand 'round with the right-hand gent."

2

She now gives left hand to her own partner and turns
  around with him .... 8 counts

> "Left hand 'round with the partner."

3

She now moves to the center of the set while the others
  join hands and circle left around her .... 16 counts

> "Lady in the center and seven hands 'round."

4

G^1 exchanges places with B^1 and the circle continues
  to move to the left .... 8 counts

> "Lady step out and gent step in."

5

B^1 leaves the center of the circle and swings his own
  partner to place while all couples swing .... 8 counts

> "Gent step out and give lady a swing."

6

Allemande left and a grand right and left.
  Continue with each successive girl leading.

JIG FIGURE 10

TO THE TUNE OF "Irish Washerwoman"

CALL

"First couple out and swing in the middle.
Shake your big feet to the tune of the fiddle.
When you get there remember my call.
Swing on the corner and promenade all."

1

Couple I swing in the middle of the set . . . . 8 counts

"First couple out and swing in the middle.
Shake your big feet to the tune of the fiddle."

2

Each boy swings the lady at his left . . . . 8 counts

"When you get there remember my call.
Swing on the corner and promenade all."

3

All promenade with this new partner around the set
and back to the boys' places . . . . 16 counts
B¹ repeats this figure three times, each time swinging a new partner. The whole dance repeats with each successive couple leading.

JIG FIGURE 11

TO THE TUNE OF "From a Man to a Jug" or "Gold Mine in the Sky"

CALL

"Gents to the center and back to the bar.
Ladies to the center and form a star.
All four gents to the right of the ring.
Go once and a quarter and then you swing."

1

Boys forward and back . . . . 8 counts

"Gents to the center and back to the bar."

2

Girls form a right-hand star in the center, turn once
around and fall back to places .... 8 counts

"Ladies to the center and form a star."

3

Boys pass behind their own partners on to the right
and swing with the next girl .... 16 counts

"All four gents to the right of the ring.
Go once and a quarter and then you swing."

4

All promenade once around the set, returning to the
boys' places .... 16 counts
The dance repeats three times, the last time boys swing with
their original partners.

JIG FIGURE 12

TO THE TUNE OF "Dixie" or any good march

CALL

"First couple around the set and face out.
Second couple around the set and face out.
Third couple around the set and face out.
Fourth couple around the set and face out.
Chassé out.
Swing your own.
Swing opposite.
Swing your own.
Swing opposite.
Swing your own.
Swing opposite."

PARTNERS SWING

1

B¹ and G¹ march to the right outside the set and when
they return to place they face out away from the
center of the set .... 16 counts

2

When Couple I reaches this position, Couple II follows around the same direction going on around
Couple I and falling in line behind them .... 16 counts

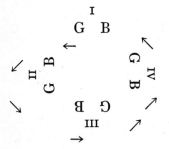 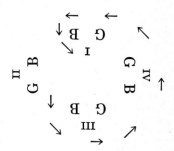

3

Couple III, do the same, falling in behind Couple II .. 16 counts

4

Couple IV follows, falling in behind Couple III...... 16 counts
The formation is now as follows:

$$B_1 \quad G_1$$
$$B_2 \quad G_2$$
$$B_3 \quad G_3$$
$$B_4 \quad G_4$$

5

Partners now face each other and step back two steps.

"Chassé out."

This leaves the dancers in the following formation:

$$B^1 \quad G^1$$
$$B^2 \quad G^2$$
$$B^3 \quad G^3$$
$$B^4 \quad G^4$$

6

B^1 and G^1 swing at the head of the set.

Then they swing with G^2 and B^2.

B^1 and G^1 swing again.

They continue down the set, swinging first together, then with the next couple, until they reach the foot of the set. This takes about 32 counts of music.

Figure 6 is repeated with Couples II, III, and IV leading in turn.

When all are back to their positions in a column of two's, Couple I leads off and the others follow.

> "Promenade away.
> You know where and I don't care."

Jig Figure 13

SUGGESTED MUSIC: "Turkey in the Straw" or "Kingdom Coming"

CALL

"First couple balance and swing.
Down the center and split the ring.
Lady go right and the gent go left.
Swing when you meet.
Swing at the head and swing at the feet.
Down the center as you did before.
Down the center and cast off four."

"Swing when you meet.
Swing at the head and swing at the feet.
Down the center as you used to do.
Down the center and cast off two.
Swing when you meet.
Swing at the head and swing at the feet.
Everybody swing.
Allemande left as pretty as you can.
Why in the world don't you right and left grand?
Meet your partner with an elbow swing,
And keep right on with the same old thing."

1

B^1 and G^1 swing in place, then chassé down the set
and pass between B^3 and G^3, B^1 turning left and
G^1 to the right .... 8 counts

"First couple balance and swing.
Down the center and split the ring.
Lady go right and gent go left."

2

They return outside the set to their places at the head,
meet and swing .... 16 counts
At the same time Couple III swings.
"Swing as you meet.
Swing at the head and swing at the feet."

3

B^1 and G^1 chassé again down the center and turn left and right
respectively, B^1 passing between Couples III and IV and G^1
between Couples II and III.

"Down the center as you did before.
Down the center and cast off four."

4

Repeat 2.

5

B ^{1} and G ^{1} chassé down the center and turn left and right respectively, B ^{1} passing between B ^{4} and G ^{4}, and G ^{1} passing between B ^{2} and G ^{2}.

> "Down the center as you used to do.
> Down the center and cast off two."

6

Repeat 2.

7

All swing partners .... 8 counts

> "Everybody swing."

8

Allemande left and a grand right and left. When partners meet each other the first time during the grand right and left they hook right elbows and turn around, then continue on around the set to places, hooking elbows and turning with the dancers they meet instead of taking hands, right then left, etc.

> "Allemande left as pretty as you can.
> Why in the world don't you right and left grand?
> Meet your partner with an elbow swing,
> And keep right on with the same old thing."

Jig Figure 14

This is an excellent march figure. Any good march may be played for it. Sets should be arranged so that they are in line with each other, both across and lengthwise of the floor. It is not satisfactory to indicate counts for the figures, because the size of the floor in each individual case will determine that.

1

Couple I marches counter-clockwise once around the set and finishes in a position facing outward, toward the head of the hall.

Couples II, III, and IV do likewise in turn, passing around Couple I and falling in line behind them. This places all sets of dancers into a double file with Couple I of Set I leading. If there are sets crosswise of the floor there will be an equal number of double files of dancers facing the head of the hall. They will also execute the figures as described below.

2

They march to the head of the hall; there they counter-march, girls to the right and boys to the left, and march to the foot of the hall.

3

Partners meet in turn and march down the center of the floor again in twos to the head of the hall. Alternating couples turn left and right respectively, and counter-march to the foot of the hall; form fours and march to head.

4

Fours counter-march to the foot of the hall; form eights and march to original places.

5

After all sets are in place, the dancers of each set join hands and circle left. This is followed by allemande left and swing partners.

The whole march may be repeated crosswise of the floor with Couples II and IV leading.

WALTZ QUADRILLE I

MUSIC: any good Waltz

FIRST CHANGE

1

Honors to corners	4 measures
Honors to partners	4 measures

2

Couples I and III forward and back, waltzing steps	8 measures

3

Couples I and III waltz with partners once around the set	8 measures

4

Each boy of Couples I and III turns to the girl at his left and waltzes with her once around the set.	8 measures
Repeat 1, 2, 3 and 4 with the side couples	32 measures

SECOND CHANGE

1

Four girls waltz to the center. Join right hands and waltz half-way around circle, finishing by stepping into position at the side of the boy opposite her own partner	8 measures

2

Boys do likewise, finishing at the side of their own
  partners .... 8 measures

3

Repeat 1 and 2. This brings all back to original
  places .... 16 measures

4

All waltz .... 32 measures

THIRD CHANGE

1

Grand right and left (waltz step) .... 16 measures

2

Couple I waltz around the outside of the set ...... 16 measures
Couples II, III, IV do likewise in succession ...... 48 measures

3

Couples I and III change partners and waltz .... 16 measures
Couples II and IV likewise .... 16 measures

4

All waltz around the room with partners as long as desired.

WALTZ QUADRILLE II

First change is the same as for Waltz Quadrille I

SECOND CHANGE

CALL

"First couple down center and there they divide.
The ladies go right and the gents go left.
Honor your partner and don't be afraid,
Swing the corner lady and waltz promenade."

1 (8 MEASURES)

Couple I joining inside hands advance with waltzing steps to Couple III and pass between boy and girl of Couple III.

"First couple down center and there they divide."

The boy turns to his left, the girl to her right, each returning outside the set to original places.

"The ladies go right and the gents go left."

2 (8 MEASURES)

Each couple salute .... 4 measures

"Honor your partner and don't be afraid."

Each boy turns to girl at his left and swings her, keeping her for his new partner .... 4 measures

"Swing the corner lady and waltz promenade."

3 (8 MEASURES)

All waltz once around the set back to boys' original places.
The dance repeats until girls are with original partners.
Third change like third change of Waltz Quadrille **I**.

CONTRA DANCES

DEVIL'S DREAM

ARRANGED BY ROBERT T. BENFORD

THE DEVIL'S DREAM

Formation—See Diagram

B^1 G^2 G^3 G^4 G^5 G^6

Head   Foot

B^6 B^5 B^4 B^3 B^2 G^1

The boy and girl of the head couple always cross over before beginning the dance.

1

B^1 and G^1 step back one step and slip down the out-
side of set . . . . 8 counts
Back . . . . 8 counts
At the same time B^6 and G^6 join hands and slip up the center and back.

2

B^6 and G^6 up the outside and back
                              while . . . . 16 counts
B^1 and G^1 down the center and back.

3

Ladies chain, Couple I and Couple II . . . . 16 counts

4

B^1 and G^1 cast off one couple. B^2 and G^1 right and
left with G^2 and B^1 . . . . 16 counts

The dance repeats until Couple I reaches the foot of the set.
Then Couple II becomes the head couple and the dance repeats over and over.

141

FIREMAN'S DANCE

ARRANGED BY ROBERT T. BENFORD

FIREMAN'S DANCE

Formation—In sets of four couples in two lines facing, the sets arranged consecutively across the room according to diagram, one set being back to back with the sets on either side.

G^1 B^1 G^3 B^3
B^2 G^2 B^4 G^4 Set   I
G^1 B^1 G^3 B^3
B^2 G^2 B^4 G^4 Set   II
G^1 B^1 G^3 B^3
B^2 G^2 B^4 G^4 Set III

1
B^2 and G^1 move back a step and slip, walk, or chassé
   down the outside of set and back

                while .... 16 counts

B^3 and G^4 join hands and slip down the center and
   back.

2
B^2 and G^1 join hands and slip down the center and
   back

                while .... 16 counts

B^3 and G^4 separate and slip up the outside and back.

3
Couples I and II ladies chain

                while .... 16 counts

Couples III and IV right and left.

4

Couples III and IV ladies chain

while .... 16 counts

Couples I and II right and left.

5

All forward and back, slow walking steps .... 8 counts

Forward again and pass through to meet a new couple

of the next set .... 8 counts

Thus one line in each set is constantly moving down the room; the other up the room. When a line of couples progresses to the outside of the room, each boy turns the girl beside him half around and waits one dance through, beginning again with the next advancing line.

FIREMAN'S DANCE

FISHER'S HORNPIPE

ARRANGED BY ROBERT T. BENFORD

FISHER'S HORNPIPE

Formation—Two lines facing, girls on one side, boys on the other; six couples making the set.

$$G^1 \ G^2 \ G^3 \ G^4 \ G^5 \ G^6$$

$$B^6 \ B^5 \ B^4 \ B^3 \ B^2 \ B^1$$

1

B¹ and G¹ step back one step and chassé down the outside of set .... 8 counts

"First couple down the outside"

Back .... 8 counts

"Back"

2

B¹ and G¹ join hands and chassé down the center .. 8 counts

"Down the center"

Back .... 8 counts

"Back"

3

B¹, with walking steps, passes behind B², while G¹ does the same with G² .... 8 counts

"Cast off one"

Couples I, II, III join hands and circle once around left .... 8 counts

"Six hands round"

4

Couples II and I right and left, finishing with Couple I in second place .... 16 counts

The dance repeats over and over from the beginning, Couple I casting off one couple each time until reaching the foot of the set. After Couple I has cast off three couples, Couple II starts at the head, etc.

MONEY MUSK

ARRANGED BY ROBERT T. BENFORD

THE MONEY MUSK

Formation—Contra-dance for 6 couples or for as many as wish, every fourth couple dancing the same as the first couple.

1

Foot

$G^6 \rightarrow$ $\leftarrow B^6$ Boy and girl of Couple I join both hands
$G^5 \rightarrow$ $\leftarrow B^5$ and swing once and a half around
$G^4 \rightarrow$ $\leftarrow B^4$ to the left in the center of the set, fin-
$G^3 \rightarrow$ $\leftarrow B^3$ ishing with the girl between B^2 and
$G^2 \rightarrow$ $\leftarrow B^2$ B^3 and the boy between G^2 and G^3 .. 8 counts
$G^1 \rightarrow$ $\leftarrow B^1$

Head

2

G^1 join hands with B^2 and B^3; B^1 with G^2 and G^3;
and the six advance to the center and back ...... 8 counts

3

B^1 and G^1 advance to the center, swing three-fourths
circle left, finishing with G^1 between B^3 and G^3 and
B^1 between B^2 and G^2 .... 8 counts

4

Forward six and back, moving up and down the set.. 8 counts

5

B^1 and G^1 advance again and swing three-quarters of
a circle left, finishing with G^1 between G^2 and G^3
and B^1 between B^2 and B^3 .... 8 counts
(By so doing Couple II has been "cast off.")

(Continued on p. 151)

OPERA REEL

ARRANGED BY ROBERT T. BENFORD

6

Couples II and I right and left .... 16 counts

This right and left is always executed with the couple which has just been "cast off."

The dance repeats over and over from the beginning.

After Couple I has cast off three couples, Couple II begins at the head, etc.

OPERA REEL

CALL

"Outside heads.
Back.
Down the center.
Back.
Cast off one
and
Right and left.
Balance in the center."

Formation—Contra-dance for eight couples

$$G^1 \; G^2 \; G^3 \; G^4 \; G^5 \; G^6 \; G^7 \; G^8$$

Head   Foot

$$B^8 \; B^7 \; B^6 \; B^5 \; B^4 \; B^3 \; B^2 \; B^1$$

1

B^1 and G^1 step back one step and slip down the outside of set .... 8 counts

"Outside heads"

Back .... 8 counts

"Back"

2

B¹ and G¹ join hands and slip down the center of set   8 counts
"Down the center"

Back . . . . 8 counts
"Back"

3

B¹ with walking steps, passes behind B², while G¹
   does the same with G², and the four right and left   8 counts

Return . . . . 8 counts
"Cast off one and right and left."

4

B¹ and G¹ balance in the center and swing . . . . 16 counts
"Balance in the center"

The dance repeats until Couple I reaches the foot of set, casting off one couple each time. After Couple I has cast off three couples, Couple II starts, etc.

FOUR IN A LINE

THE REEL

SUGGESTED MUSIC: "Drunken Sailor"

The dance may be executed with either skipping or walking steps.

Formation

Foot

$B^4 \rightarrow \quad \leftarrow G^4$ Four couples, one behind another, all facing line
$G^3 \rightarrow \quad \leftarrow B^3$ of direction. In the odd couples the boy stands at
$B^2 \rightarrow \quad \leftarrow G^2$ the girl's left; in the even couples the boy stands
$G^1 \rightarrow \quad \leftarrow B^1$ at the girl's right.

Head

Figure 1

1. Couple I, inside hands joined, skip down the room   8 counts
   Return . . . . 8 counts
   (In each return, individuals turn directly about, changing hands, coming back in the same path in which they advanced.)

2. Couple I now takes Couple II between them and advance down the room four in a line . . . . 8 counts
   Return . . . . 8 counts

3. Couples I and II now take Couple III between them and advance . . . . 8 counts
   Return . . . . 8 counts

4. Couples I, II, III, advance with Couple IV in the center, making a line of eight . . . . 8 counts
   Return . . . . 8 counts

153

DRUNKEN SAILOR

ARRANGED BY ROBERT T. BENFORD

Figure 2

Formation: In line of eight as in finish of Figure 1, all facing center of line.

$$\text{B}^1 \text{ G}^2 \text{ B}^3 \text{ G}^4 \qquad \text{B}^4 \text{ G}^3 \text{ B}^2 \text{ G}^1$$

With skipping steps, 16 counts, a new set is formed, B^1 and G^1 going to the foot of the set, B^2 and G^2 to the head, making the following formation for the repetition of the dance.

$$
\begin{array}{lll}
\text{B}^1 & \text{G}^1 & \text{Foot} \\
\text{G}^4 & \text{B}^4 & \\
\text{B}^3 & \text{G}^3 & \\
\text{G}^2 & \text{B}^2 & \text{Head}
\end{array}
$$

The dance is repeated in this manner until each couple has been at the head.

THE TEMPEST

ARRANGED BY ROBERT T. BENFORD

THE TEMPEST I

Formation—Eight couples in double line facing each other. There may be any number of such sets running side by side across the room. The head couple crosses over before beginning.

$$B^1 \quad G^2 \quad G^3 \quad G^4 \quad G^5 \quad G^6 \quad G^7 \quad G^8$$

Head   Foot

$$G^1 \quad B^2 \quad B^3 \quad B^4 \quad B^5 \quad B^6 \quad B^7 \quad B^8$$

1

B^1, G^2, G^1 and B^2 join hands and chassé down the
center and back, four abreast .... 16 counts

2

B^1 and G^1 balance to G^2 and B^2 .... 8 counts
Circle four .... 8 counts

3

Couples I and II, Ladies chain .... 16 counts

1

Couple I now take Couple III and chassé down the
center and back, finishing below Couple II .... 16 counts

2

Couple I balance to Couple III .... 8 counts
Circle four .... 8 counts

3

Couples I and III ladies chain .... 16 counts
Repeat over and over passing below one couple each time. When Couple I reaches the fourth couple of the set, Couple II begins the dance again at the head.

THE TEMPEST II

This form of "The Tempest" is easier than the other and is especially good to use as a "mixer" for beginners.

"All join hands and circle to the left.
Right hand star.
Left hand star.
Forward and back.
Forward again and pass through."

Formation—In sets with fours facing as in the following diagram:

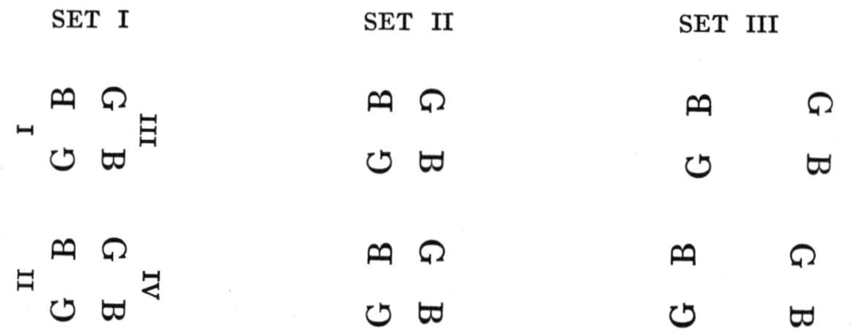

SET I	SET II	SET III
B G	B G	B G
I III		
G B	G B	G B
B G	B G	B G
II IV		
G B	G B	G B

1

All join hands and circle once left . . . . 16 counts

2

Couples I and III
            and   form a right hand star . . . . 8 counts
Couples II and IV

Repeat—forming a left hand star . . . . 8 counts

158

3

The two lines forward and back .... 8 counts

4

Lines move forward again, drop hands, and pass
through to meet another line of four .... 8 counts
The dance repeats as often as desired.

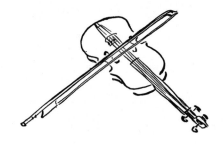

VIRGINIA REEL OR McDONALD'S REEL

ARRANGED BY ROBERT T. BENF

VIRGINIA REEL

CALL

"Head lady and foot gent forward and back.
Forward and swing with the right hand 'round.
Forward again with the left hand 'round.
Forward again with both hands 'round.
Do-si-do.
Reel.
Up the center.
Down the outside.
Form an arch and balance through."

Formation—Contra-dance for six couples

H	G^1 G^2 G^3 G^4 G^5 G^6	F
e		o
a		o
d	B^1 B^2 B^3 B^4 B^5 B^6	t

1

G^1 and B^6 advance to meet each other in the center
of the set, pay address, and move backward to place   8 counts
B^1 and G^6 do likewise . . . .   8 counts

2

G^1 and B^6 advance to meet each other, take right
hands, swing once about, and move backward to
place . . . .   8 counts
B^1 and G^6, the same . . . .   8 counts

3

Same as 2, turning with left hands . . . . 16 counts

4

Same as 2, swinging with both hands . . . . 16 counts

5

G^1 and B^6 do-si-do . . . . 8 counts
B^1 and G^6 do likewise . . . . 8 counts

6

(16 MEASURES)

Couple I execute the "reel." B^1 takes his partner's right hand in his and turns her once and a half around. G^1 now takes left hand with B^2 and turns him about, while B^1 does likewise with G^2. Couple I meet, give right hands and swing once around in the center of the set. B^1 gives left hand to G^3 and G^1 to B^3. So they continue down the set meeting with a right-hand swing below each couple, until they have reached the foot of the set.

7

B^1 and G^1 join both hands and chassé up the center to the head; then counter-march to the foot, all couples following . . . . 16 counts

8

B^1 and G^1 form an arch and each successive couple
joins both hands and chassé through the arch to
place, leaving Couple I at the foot of the set ..... 32 counts
The dance repeats until each couple has been at the head.
Then all move forward and back .... 8 counts
Forward again; partners swing and promenade away.

THE CAMPBELLS ARE COMING

ARRANGED BY ROBERT T. BENFORD

SCOTCH REEL

TO THE TUNE OF: "The Campbells Are Coming"

Formation—A circle of sets of four, the two couples in each set facing each other, as in Sicilian Circle

CALL

"Partners with the right hand 'round.
Partners with the left hand 'round.
Balance four.
Ladies chain.
Right and left.
Forward and back.
Forward again and pass through."

1

Partners give right hands and swing once around ...   8 counts

2

Repeat with left hands ....   8 counts

3

Two couples balance four ....   16 counts

4

Ladies chain ....   16 counts

5

Right and left ....   16 counts

6

Forward and back ....   8 counts

7

Forward again and pass through to meet a new couple   8 counts
The dance repeats as long as desired.

GUILDEROY REEL

MUSIC: "Guilderoy Reel" or any good reel

This dance is generally done with the "chassé" step, but the brisk walking step may be used.

Formation—Six couples in two lines, partners facing, as in Fisher's Hornpipe.

1

B^1 and G^1 taking G^2 between them advance down the
center of the set . . . .   8 counts

2

Leaving G^2 at the foot of the set, Couple I returns to
place . . . .   8 counts

3 and 4

Repeat 1 and 2 taking B^2 . . . .   16 counts

5

B^1 and G^1 each steps back of his line and moves with
sliding steps down to the foot of the set . . . .   8 counts

6

They return, hands joined, up the center of the set to original places, followed by Couple II.

7

On reaching original places, Couples I and II right
and left . . . .   16 counts

The first couple slides to the foot of the set as Couple II begins the dance again.

Continue as long as desired.

NEW CENTURY HORNPIPE

MUSIC: "New Century Hornpipe" or any good hornpipe

Formation—Six couples in two lines, partners facing, as in Fisher's Hornpipe. There may be as many sets of six couples as desired.

1

B^1 and G^1 balance on the head of the set . . . .   4 counts

2

B^1 and G^1 join both hands and swing once and a half
around, finishing in opposite places . . . .   12 counts

3

Couples I and II ladies chain . . . .   16 counts

4

B^1 and G^1 balance in the center of the set . . . .   4 counts

5

Couple I swings again once and a half, finishing one
place below Couple II . . . .   12 counts
(This "casts off" Couple II leaving them at the head of the
set.)

6

Couples II and I right and left . . . .   16 counts
Couple I repeats the dance until they have reached the foot of the set. After three couples have been "cast off," the new head couple starts in the same way. The dance may continue as long as is desired.

CIRCLE DANCES

THE CIRCLE

ARRANGED BY ROBERT T. BENFORD

SICILIAN CIRCLE

MUSIC: "The Circle"

Formation—Sets of four in double circle around the room, the two couples in each set, facing each other.

1
Couples forward and back .... 8 counts

2
Four join hands and circle once left .... 8 counts

3
Ladies chain .... 16 counts

4
Right and left .... 16 counts

5
Promenade across and back .... 16 counts

LADIES CHANGE

6

Forward and back . . . .   8 counts

Forward and pass through to meet a new couple . . . .   8 counts

   The dance repeats over and over, couples advancing around the circle.

WILD IRISHMAN I

MUSIC: "Irish Washerwoman"

Formation—Quadrille with an odd dancer in the center of the set.

CALL

"Wild Irishman swing at the head.
Wild Irishman swing at the foot.
Allemande left.
Grand right and left.
Wild Irishman swing on the side.
Wild Irishman swing on the side.
Allemande left.
Grand right and left."

1

The odd dancer swings with the girl of Couple I . . . .   8 counts

Then with girl of Couple III . . . .   8 counts

     "Wild Irishman swing at the head.
     Wild Irishman swing at the foot."

2

Allemande left . . . .   8 counts

Grand right and left . . . . 16 counts

IRISH WASHERWOMAN

ARRANGED BY ROBERT T. BENFORD

3

Repeat 1 with Couples II and IV . . . . 16 counts

> "Wild Irishman swing on the side.
> Wild Irishman swing on the side."

4

Repeat 2 . . . . 24 counts

As 4 is being danced the "Wild Irishman" works in and attempts to secure a partner in the set.

The dance continues over and over as long as desired.

WILD IRISHMAN II

CALLER'S SONG

"My mother and father were Irish,
My mother and father were Irish,
My mother and father were Irish and I am Irish too."

"The right hand to your partner,
The left hand to your neighbor,
The right hand to your partner and all promenade."

Formation—Single circle, facing center. One odd boy in the center.

1

All join hands and circle to the left . . . . 16 counts

2

Boys take partner's right hand and pass by . . . . 4 counts

> "The right hand to your partner."

Boys then turn girls whom they meet half around with
the left hand .... 4 counts

"The left hand to your neighbor."

Boys turn own partner again with right hand ...... 4 counts

"The right hand to your partner."

Girls take partner's arm for a promenade .... 4 counts

"And all promenade."

3

Partners promenade around the circle .... 16 counts
The odd boy tries to secure a partner during the change of
hands, and the dance repeats over and over from the beginning.

PAUL JONES

MUSIC: Any lively march or two-step

The "Paul Jones" is frequently used at the beginning of a
dancing party as a social mixer. It brings about a frequent change
of partners and creates a great deal of fun. It may be continued as
long as desired. In conducting a "Paul Jones" the "caller" uses
his own originality in the succession of changes. The following are
examples of a possible sequence of the most common changes used
in the dance.

1. Couples march about the room in twos, then fours.
2. All join hands and circle to the left; to the right.
3. All forward and back.
4. Right hands to partners and a grand right and left.
5. All two-step or swing.

6. Ladies form a circle in the center, gentlemen on the outside.
7. Ladies circle to the left, and gentlemen to the right.
8. All two-step or swing.
9. All march in twos about the room.
10. March four abreast.
11. While marching four abreast, gentlemen stand still and ladies advance, passing a given number of groups, then all promenade again; or ladies stand still and gentlemen pass on a given number of groups.
12. Change partners in fours and swing or two-step.

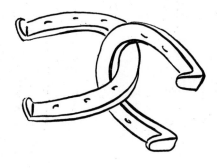

COUPLE DANCES

FROM A MAN TO A JUG

ARRANGED BY ROBERT T. BENFORD

POLKA A

SUGGESTED MUSIC: "From a Man to a Jug" or any good polka

Formation—In couples, boy standing somewhat behind and at the left of girl.

Boy holds girl's left hand in his, arms extended sideward, and her right hand in his at her right hip.

1

1. Touch left heel sideward	1	count
Touch left toe to right foot	1	count
2. Two-step, boy and girl changing sides	2	counts
Repeat 1 and 2 starting right	4	counts
Repeat all	8	counts

2

1. Starting with left foot take four slides left	4	counts
2. Repeat, going right	4	counts
Repeat 1 and 2	8	counts

Repeat the dance over and over.

POLKA B

MUSIC: Same as for Polka A

Formation—Partners facing, hands joined, arms extended sideward. Boy starts with left foot, girl with right.

(Description for boy)

1

1. Touch left heel sidewards	1	count
Touch left toe to right foot	1	count
2. Two-step left	2	counts
Repeat 1 and 2 right	4	counts
Repeat all	8	counts

POLK

2

Take partner in regular dance position and two-step   8 measures
Repeat all, over and over.

THE RACQUET

MUSIC: "Captain Jinks"

Formation—Couples, in regular dance position

(Description for boy)

1

4 slides right	4 counts
4 slides left	4 counts
1 two-step right	2 counts
1 two-step left	2 counts
Boys turn partners completely around right	4 counts

2

Partners two-step for 16 counts

THE RYE WALTZ

ARRANGED BY ROBERT T. BENFORD

THE RYE WALTZ

MUSIC: "The Rye Waltz"

Formation—In couples, waltz position
(Description for boy; girl same, starting with opposite foot)

1

1. Point left toe sideward	1 count
Point left toe slightly in front of right foot	1 count
Repeat (1)	2 counts
2. 3 sides left. Point right on fourth count	4 counts
Repeat 1 and 2 starting right	8 counts
Repeat all	16 counts

2

Waltz for 16 measures

COMING THROUGH THE RYE

MUSIC: "The Rye Waltz"

Formation—In couples, the boy standing somewhat behind
and at the left of the girl. Boy holds girl's left hand in his, arms
extended sideward, and her right hand in his at her right hip.

1

1. Point left toe sideward	1 count
Bring left foot back to position and transfer weight to it	1 count
Same right	2 counts

THE RYE WALTZ

2. 3 slides left, finishing with right toe pointed ..... 4 counts
Repeat 1 and 2 starting right .... 8 counts
Repeat all .... 16 counts

2

Partners take waltz position and waltz .... 16 measures

OXFORD WALTZ

In this dance, as in the "Rye Waltz," the first part is done in polka time and the second part in waltz time. If the music for "Oxford" is not available, the same music used for the "Rye Waltz" may be used.

Formation—Couples. Partners side by side with inside hands joined.

The descriptions for parts 1 and 2 are for the boy. The girl's part is the same only she uses the opposite foot.

1

Walk three steps forward beginning with the left foot
and finish pointing the right toe forward .... 4 counts
Repeat, starting with the right foot and finishing with
the left toe pointed .... 4 counts

2

Partners face each other. Join hands.
Step left .... 1 count
Point right toe across left .... 2 counts
Step right .... 3 counts
Point left toe across right .... 4 counts
Repeat the above .... 4 counts
Repeat 1 and 2 .... 16 counts

3

Partners take waltzing position and waltz .... 16 measures

SCHOTTISCHE

ARRANGED BY ROBERT T. BENFORD

SCHOTTISCHE

SCHOTTISCHE A

Formation—as in Polka A

1

One schottische step forward beginning right .... 4 counts
One schottische step forward beginning left .... 4 counts
 (The barn dance schottische step is used here and is: step right, count 1; step left, count 2; step right, count 3; hop right swinging left foot forward, count 4.)

2

Step-hop forward, right, making a quarter turn right.. 2 counts
Step-hop backward, left, making a quarter turn left.. 2 counts
Repeat above .... 4 counts

 Repeat all as often as desired.

SCHOTTISCHE B

Formation—In couples, partners side by side, the boy's right hand at the back of girl's waist, her left hand resting on his right shoulder.

(Description for boy; girl same, on opposite foot)

1

Schottische forward, beginning left .... 4 counts
Schottische forward, beginning right .... 4 counts

2

Partners take regular dance position and the boy turns
 partner completely around with step-hops, starting
 with the left foot .... 8 counts
 Repeat over and over from beginning.

SCHOTTISCHE

VARSOVIENNE

ARRANGED BY ROBERT T. BENFORD

VARSOVIENNE

MUSIC: "Varsovienne"

Formation—In couples, boy standing somewhat behind and at the left of girl.

1

1. Swing left foot across right	1 count
Step left	1 count
Draw right foot up to left foot and transfer weight to it	1 count
Repeat	3 counts
2. Swing left foot across right	1 count
Girl and boy change sides with a step left and a step right	2 counts
Step left	1 count
Point right toe sideward and hold	2 counts
Repeat 1 and 2, starting right	12 counts

2

1. Swing left foot across right	1 count
Girl and boy change sides with a step left and a step right, girl passing in front of boy	2 counts
Step left	1 count
Point right toe sideward and hold	2 points
Repeat 1 starting right	6 counts
Repeat 1 starting left	6 counts
Girl turns to face boy. Couple take waltz position	6 counts

3

Partners waltz .... 8 measures

The dance repeats over and over from the beginning.

The dance may also be done just the same in regular dance position, the above description being for boy; the girl starting with the opposite foot.

The following change will need to be made:

Part 2 of 1, boy swings partner completely around... 3 counts
Boy steps left .... 1 count
Boy points right, girl left .... 2 counts

The following song is often used with the dance:
"Have You Seen My New Shoes"

> Have you seen my,
> Have you seen my,
> Have you seen my new shoes?
>
> With their bows on,
> With their bows on,
> With their bows on the toes.
>
> Have you seen my new shoes
> With their bows on the toes?
> Have you seen my new shoes
> With their bows on the toes?

INDEX